OXFORD CHILDREN'S REFERENCE LIBRARY

THE ARAB WORLD

OXFORD CHILDREN'S REFERENCE LIBRARY

General Editors: Patrick Moore and Laura E. Salt

Oxford Children's Reference Library

13

THE ARAB WORLD

by

SHIRLEY KAY

illustrated by

ULRICA LLOYD

OXFORD UNIVERSITY PRESS

1970

Oxford University Press, Ely House, London W.1

GLASGOW NEW YORK TORONTO MELBOURNE WELLINGTON
CAPE TOWN DELHI IBADAN NAIROBI DAR ES SALAAM LUSAKA ADDIS ABABA
BOMBAY CALCUTTA MADRAS KARACHI LAHORE DACCA
KUALA LUMPUR SINGAPORE HONG KONG TOKYO

First published 1970
Reprinted with corrections 1975

PRINTED IN GREAT BRITAIN BY W. S. COWELL LTD, AT THE BUTTER MARKET, IPSWICH

CONTENTS

INTRODUCTION

THIS BOOK IN THE Oxford Children's Reference Library describes that part of the world in which the Arabs live — the Arabian Peninsula where they started; the north of Africa including Egypt; and the countries of the Middle East (excepting Israel), as far as Iraq. For several hundred years, until the last century, Europeans knew very little about the Arabs and scarcely ever visited Arab lands. This is not very surprising since the Arabs live in some of the hottest places in the world, and it was not easy for Europeans to stay alive there. Also the desert, which makes up much of the Arab world, was inhabited by fierce tribes who enjoyed fighting each other and were always ready to attack foreigners too. Only a few daring explorers undertook the exciting adventure of visiting Arab lands. Among these were Richard Burton and Charles Doughty, whose stories are told in Book 2 of this series.

People knew more about the Arabs in the middle ages, for then they were a powerful people, who spread far and wide and settled in parts of southern Europe, especially Spain. They had great universities and knew many things which the Europeans did not know. Europeans learnt from the Arabs the Arabic numbers which we use today, how to make paper, how to study the stars, and a great deal about science and medicine. Also the Arabs ruled the lands of the Bible and the towns where Jesus had lived. In 1095, after the Turks had begun to conquer the Arab lands, many Europeans went on Crusades (see Chapter 17) to rescue the Holy Places. For about 200 years, they lived in the Arab lands and brought back from Arab traders good things such as sugar, spices, and beautiful woven materials.

Nowadays Europeans are once again interested in Arab countries, mainly because there is more oil under the Arab deserts than anywhere else in the world. In the modern world oil is very important. We need it to make our machines work; from oil we get petrol to drive our cars and aeroplanes, and lorries and trains use diesel oil; we need tar, a form of oil, for building our roads. The modern world would come to a stand-still without oil. So Europeans go to live in the Arab deserts to look for this oil and to bring it up out of the ground.

In many parts of the Arab world people still live the poor, hard life of the desert. But in other places money from oil and trade has made the people rich and able to build big modern cities. This book tells us how all this has come to pass: how the few desert tribes in Arabia, inspired by their prophet Muhammad, conquered the countries we now call the Arab world and made them Arab too; how they became rich and powerful, then poor again; and how oil has now brought them extraordinary riches.

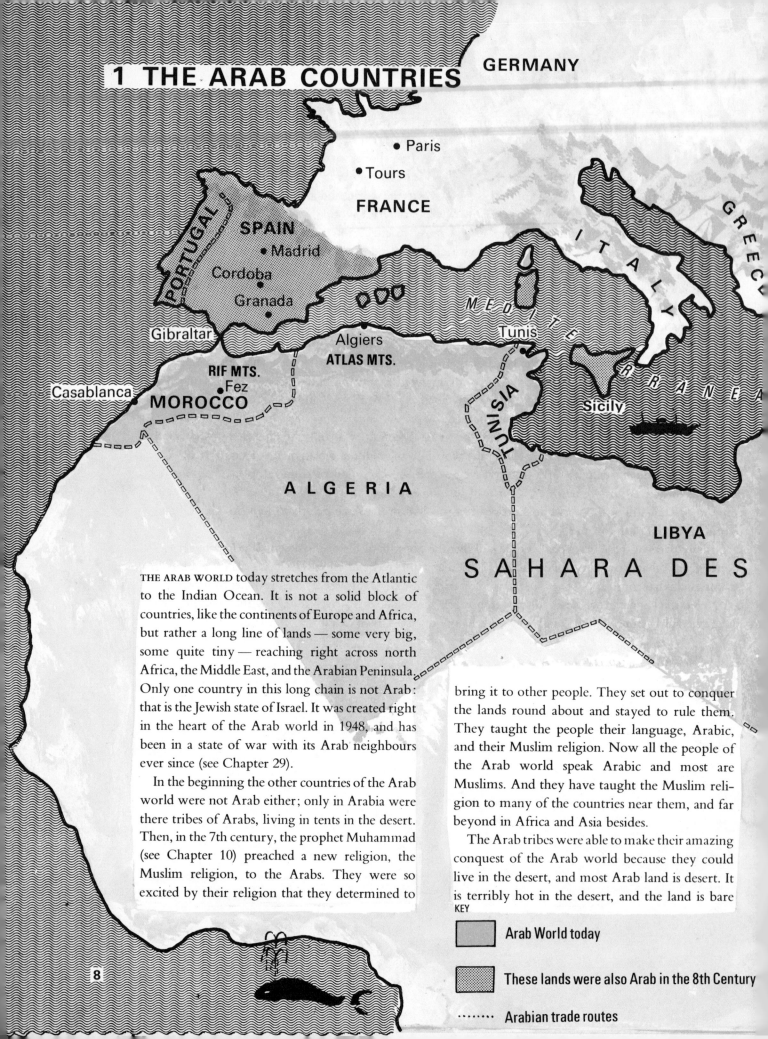

1 THE ARAB COUNTRIES

GERMANY

• Paris

• Tours

FRANCE

SPAIN

PORTUGAL

• Madrid

Cordoba

Granada

Gibraltar

Algiers

ATLAS MTS.

RIF MTS.

Casablanca

Fez

MOROCCO

ITALY

GREECE

MEDITERRANEAN

Tunis

TUNISIA

Sicily

ALGERIA

LIBYA

SAHARA DES

THE ARAB WORLD today stretches from the Atlantic to the Indian Ocean. It is not a solid block of countries, like the continents of Europe and Africa, but rather a long line of lands — some very big, some quite tiny — reaching right across north Africa, the Middle East, and the Arabian Peninsula. Only one country in this long chain is not Arab: that is the Jewish state of Israel. It was created right in the heart of the Arab world in 1948, and has been in a state of war with its Arab neighbours ever since (see Chapter 29).

In the beginning the other countries of the Arab world were not Arab either; only in Arabia were there tribes of Arabs, living in tents in the desert. Then, in the 7th century, the prophet Muhammad (see Chapter 10) preached a new religion, the Muslim religion, to the Arabs. They were so excited by their religion that they determined to

bring it to other people. They set out to conquer the lands round about and stayed to rule them. They taught the people their language, Arabic, and their Muslim religion. Now all the people of the Arab world speak Arabic and most are Muslims. And they have taught the Muslim religion to many of the countries near them, and far beyond in Africa and Asia besides.

The Arab tribes were able to make their amazing conquest of the Arab world because they could live in the desert, and most Arab land is desert. It is terribly hot in the desert, and the land is bare

KEY

Arab World today

These lands were also Arab in the 8th Century

.... Arabian trade routes

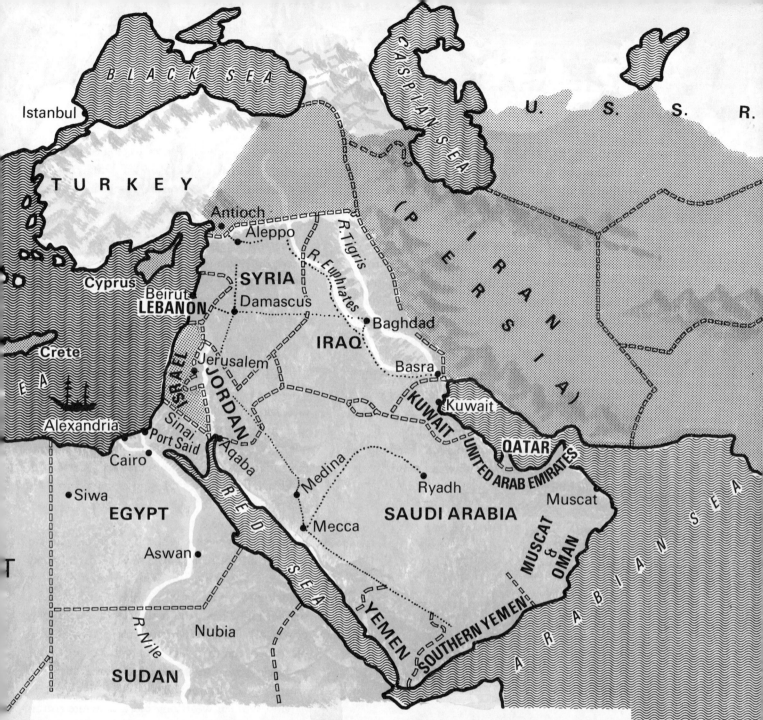

sand and rock (see Chapters 3 and 4). There are few plants and almost no water. But the Arabs had a great desert animal, the camel, which can go into the most barren desert and live for days without food or water. Riding their camels, the Arabs could travel long distances across the deserts, to conquer other countries.

Apart from desert tribes, people can live in the Arab world only where they can find enough water. Most of the big cities today are built on the coast, or on one of the big rivers such as the Nile, the Tigris, and the Euphrates (see Chapters 20 and 33). These rivers were important to man long before the Arabs came, for the earliest civilizations in the world started there (see Book 12). Other towns and villages are built in oases (see Chapter 5) in the desert, where water comes from springs or wells. Nowadays new desert towns are built where oil is found (see Chapter 25), but they, too, must have water.

2 THE ARABS

A farmer and his wife

WHAT IS AN ARAB? Is he a Bedouin Sheikh in his turban and long white gown proudly riding his thoroughbred Arab horse; or a smooth shopkeeper wearing a white skullcap, who pops out of his booth to persuade a foreigner to pay twice the value for his carpet or leather bag? Or is he the baggy-trousered workman asleep on the corner of the pavement and not bothered at all whether he finishes his work today, tomorrow, or never; or the government official in his smart European suit, sitting behind his desk in an air-conditioned office, and greeting his visitor in perfect English? Or perhaps we mean the *fellah*, or peasant, with his dirty white cotton garment drawn up between his legs, and a strip of white cotton wrapped round his head; he is riding a donkey, while his wife, in a long black robe, walks behind carrying the bundles; or he is drawing up water from the river to water his crops.

All these people are Arabs, to be seen in almost any part of the Arab world and, although they are so different, they have certain things in common — most important, their language, Arabic, and their religion, Islam.

The first Arabs were wandering tribes in the deserts of Arabia who sent their camel caravans to trade with neighbouring countries. Then in the 7th century, inspired by the teaching of Muhammad, they left their own desert and spread all over what we now call 'the Arab world' and far beyond (see Chapter 12). Wherever they went they married with the women of the countries they conquered. So now the Arabs are a very mixed race. Most have light-brown skins, dark eyes, and straight black hair, and are usually rather slight and not very tall. But the descendants of those who inter-married with Negroes may have dark skins and black frizzy hair, while those whose ancestors married with European or other races may have fair hair and blue eyes.

Most Arabs wear clothes suited to the climate they live in. The men protect their heads and necks from the scorching sun with white turbans or headcloths kept in place by a black cord, or just a strip of rag. They protect their bodies with long gowns or with baggy cotton trousers hanging in pleats between their legs. But today many Arabs in the cities wear the same sort of clothes that men wear in cities all over the world.

Most women wear long black or white cotton robes covering them from head to toe, and these keep off the heat of the sun. In many Arab countries women are not allowed out of doors with their faces uncovered; they must wear veils which vary from place to place. In the desert the veil may be a leather mask with slits for the eyes. In other places the black or white robe goes over the face. In Jordan the women sometimes have black veils with coloured flowers painted on them. In Algeria a white veil is wrapped so that only one eye remains uncovered, or a little lace-trimmed triangle

An Arab Sheikh from Iraq

it is more important than to many people to save face. So, for example, if two cars bump into each other in a town, it is more likely to result in a row.

Governments also feel that they lose authority if they admit a mistake, which is partly why it is difficult for them to make peace with Israel. Honour to them is more important than anything, even more important than practical considerations.

Life in the desert where each tribe was its own master made Arabs independent, and still to this day they do not work easily with anyone else, and even worse for anyone else. They talk about Arab unity, but have not yet managed to make it work. But in spite of this they do think of each other as brothers, and they do have a similar way of judging the world around them.

of material is tied over the nose and mouth. At home a woman can take off her veil, unless men visitors come to the house, and in the desert she may usually go unveiled, for there are no strangers to see her. In the big cities many women are gaining more freedom in other ways, and may go unveiled and wear European clothing.

The rule about veils is but one of the many rules which make up the Arab code of honour. Most of these rules have come from the times when most Arabs lived in the desert, and an Arab's honour depended on his ability to fight to defend his family, guests, and land. The shame of failing in this was so great that he could only recover his honour by seeking revenge. Every Arab belonged to a tribe, a group of related families, and his honour was the concern of the tribe. So the tribes were constantly fighting each other. Today the law forbids tribes to fight or raid each other's villages, but the ideas of honour still remain — even in the cities. No one likes admitting that he is in the wrong, but Arabs, especially the less well-educated ones, find it particularly difficult, since to Arabs

All these people are from different parts of the Arab World

3 THE DESERT 1

MOST ARAB LAND is desert, a hot, dry world where almost nothing grows or moves, and there is no noise. There are deserts elsewhere in the world, but the largest, hottest deserts are in the Arab world. To the Arabs the desert is home; they came from the desert, and their way of life is the desert way.

In summer the desert is as hot as a furnace. The sand is so hot that it burns one's feet. The few people who live in the desert sit still under their tents, and roll up the side flaps to catch the slightest breeze. People who live in tents in the desert are called Bedouin, from an Arab word *badawi*, meaning 'desert-dwellers' (see Chapter 6). The highest temperature measured anywhere in the world was in the Sahara: 58°C. in the shade!

But in winter the desert can be very cold. An English explorer of the Empty Quarter in Arabia described how his feet were frozen when he walked on the cold sand one morning, although at midday he was too hot. Even in summer, it is always cool in the desert at night, for as soon as the sun sets, the land cools very quickly. The sky is very clear, and the stars look brilliant and very close.

The wind blows fiercely across the desert for there are no trees to break its force. Sometimes a strong wind lifts the sand and whirls it along in a fearful sandstorm. Then men lie down behind their camels with their backs to the wind, cover their faces, and wait for the storm to blow itself out. They find it hard to breathe, for their mouths and eyes fill with grit. The sand blows over everything, wiping out tracks and burying landmarks, and then a traveller may easily lose his way and perhaps die. Such sandstorms cause the sand dunes to move, shifting waves of drifting sand, and the force of the driving sand chisels rocks and mountains into fantastic shapes. A car, caught in a sandstorm, may have all its paint scraped off, as though it had been rubbed with sandpaper. The wind blowing from the Sahara Desert carries hot air and even sand across the Mediterranean Sea to the south of Europe. It is feared by Europeans, who are not used to such heat.

The desert at night.
The jackals are howling at
the passing travellers

A sandstorm

Sometimes the traveller in the desert thinks he sees a lake shimmering in front of him. He goes towards it, hoping to find water, but as he comes near, the water disappears. This is called a mirage. Occasionally in summer one can see something of the same sort on an English road; a puddle appears on the hot road ahead, but when one reaches it, there is no puddle there. Mirages are caused by heat, which makes the air quiver, so that the land shimmers like water, and people think it is really water. Sometimes there are even reflections of plants and hills on it, because the heat can also make objects appear twice, once the right way up, and once upside down. The heat may also make people, camels, or cars in the distance look like spinning tops.

Until recently, the deserts were a dangerous, remote world across which only the Bedouin, and those they chose to guide, dared risk to travel. Camel caravans in the past were guided by Bedouin, who found their way by recognizing the shapes of hills or dunes; at best they had vague tracks to follow, which usually ran from one oasis to another (see Chapter 5). Desert travellers also learnt to find their direction by studying the stars. But now there are roads right across the desert, and more and more are being built. Lorries and trucks cross the Sahara regularly, and even the forbidding Empty Quarter in Arabia is no longer empty. Men have explored the remotest parts in search of oil, for a great deal of oil has been found under the desert (see Chapter 25). Also aircraft now fly over the desert, and there are airports. But in spite of this, the desert can still be a dangerous and lonely place.

4 THE DESERT 2

Dhub lizard

MOST PEOPLE THINK of the desert as wave after wave of sand dunes, such as one sees by the sea in some countries. There are great sand deserts: the largest one in the world is in Arabia, and it has the expressive name of The Empty Quarter. But more often, deserts are just bare land: maybe gravel, maybe rocks, maybe sandy soil and stones. In some places they are yellow; in others brown, red, grey, or even black where the stones littering the desert floor came from an ancient volcano, or white in the great salt flats left by dried-up pools of rain. The colour of the desert changes throughout the day: in the early morning and evening the colour is darker; at midday it may look almost white, because the sunlight is so strong.

In some parts of the desert there may be no rain for many years on end. In these places nothing grows for years; then there will be a sudden storm, causing a flash flood which may sweep away houses and cut deep channels in the ground. In other parts of the desert, where there is a little rain, dry, scrubby bushes and plants grow here and there. Everywhere, after a rain storm, plants shoot up as though by magic, flower quickly, and then die away, not to flower again perhaps for years. Only certain types of plants and animals can live in the desert, for they must be specially adapted for it.

A scorpion

The desert is not an easy home for wild animals. There is little to eat and nowhere to hide. So animals of the desert must either be able to run fast or to dig burrows underground, and they are usually fawn or cream coloured — the same colour as their background. The jerboa is a little animal, which looks like a jumping mouse and hops like a tiny kangaroo. Its body is only 20 centimetres long, but it has long back legs and a long tail which acts as a rudder when it jumps, making it able to change direction in mid-air. A number of jerboas dig burrows close together and stay underground all day, only coming out just before sunset to look for seeds and insects to eat. They can live with practically nothing to drink at all.

Another animal which lives underground in the desert is the desert fox, or fennec. Fennecs are small, creamy-coloured foxes with huge ears; they are very beautiful, and people like to keep baby ones as pets. They are not easy to catch for they, too, only come out at night, but occasionally they sneak into an oasis (see Chapter 5) for a drink of water. Larger animals, such as jackals and gazelles, also need an occasional drink. Gazelles can escape very quickly though, for they are light and delicate and have long, thin legs. Some have been known to run as fast as 60 km/h. The oryx, which is bigger, has two horns, but otherwise it looks like the legendary unicorn: indeed, stories of the oryx may have started the legend of the unicorn. If seen from the side, the oryx may have looked as though it had only one horn, and also a horn quite often breaks off. So people could easily have thought there was an animal which really had only one horn.

Fennec fox of Algeria

There are many lizards in the desert, for they like hot, dry places. Some grow 60 cm long, but most are tiny. They eat insects, and a few eat plants. Their skins are waterproof, and their bodies do not lose water by perspiring, as other animals do; so they can live in the heat. A less attractive desert creature is the scorpion, which carries a poisonous sting in its tail. It arches its tail over its back and then strikes forward with it at its victim. It catches insects in its front claws, stings them to death, then sucks them dry. It generally runs away, if it can, but to defend itself it will sting anything it meets, including people, and the sting can even kill people. Only fennecs are not hurt by the scorpion's sting.

The large desert animals are getting fewer, for they are being shot by men from cars. There is nowhere in the desert for them to hide, and the cars travel faster than they can run. Once many ostriches lived in the desert; their egg-shells are still found, but there are no ostriches now. In 1950 there were still about 1,000 oryxes in Arabia, but 15 years later there were only about ten left.

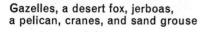
Gazelles, a desert fox, jerboas,
a pelican, cranes, and sand grouse

Some plants, like animals, are specially equipped to survive in deserts. The little flowers which come up after rain quickly produce seeds, and these seeds can last for years until there is rain again to make them grow. Desert shrubs do not grow very tall, but they have extremely long roots which collect water from a wide area. A shrub 60 cm high may have roots 6 metres long. Many shrubs have thorns to prevent animals eating them; they are tough and leathery and usually a dusty grey colour. The oleander has bright pink flowers and poisonous dark-green leaves which no animals dare eat — not even the camel, which eats most of the tough prickly little shrubs. It grows in wadis (dried-up stream beds).

15

5 THE OASIS

IN SOME PLACES in the desert there is a patch of green where plants can be grown and people can live. This is called an oasis. Palm trees grow here, and also grass on which animals can feed. People can make gardens and grow vegetables and sometimes wheat. In some oases there may be a few houses, including a caravanserai (see Chapter 16), where travellers can stay the night; in others there may be a village or even a town. The oasis in Siwa in Egypt is about 9 by 8 kilometres in area, and there are several villages. The oasis of Dakhla supports well over 20,000 people. There are usually roads, and now sometimes railways, connecting the bigger oases.

Oases can be developed only where there is water. Sometimes the water is brought by a river; then it is easy to plant crops along its banks. The oasis of Damascus in Syria (see Chapter 14) is like this. All the water from the river is used up by the great city and its gardens, which stretch for about 24 km beyond the city. Then, when there is no water left, the desert starts again. In some oases there are springs with pools of water, where it is easy to make gardens. But more often the water is underground and must be pumped to the surface and led through irrigation channels to the fields.

All is bustle and life in a big oasis: men are working the gardens, driving donkeys or camels loaded with dates, vegetables, or fuel, or working the pumps which bring water up from the wells. There is a busy market, and the Bedouin from the neighbouring desert bring their animals to trade for the produce of the oasis. They buy food and cooking pots, or rugs and coats woven by the women of the village, and then they bask in the cool, green shade of the trees while their herds are drinking at the wells. It seems like the Garden of Eden after the dry, empty desert all around. Some say the oasis of Damascus was the Garden of Eden. The Bedouin enjoy it while they can, for when they leave the oasis they must travel hundreds of kilometres before they will reach the next one. Between one oasis and another there are no houses, no trees, no grass — only desert.

The most important crop in every oasis is the date palm. Date palms grow up to 24 metres tall, with feathery leaves sprouting from the tops of their trunks. Each year the old leaves are cut off, leaving stumps, like steps, right up the trunk. Every part of the tree is used: the dates are so nourishing that people can live on them; the date stones are crushed to make food for camels; the wood is used for building; the leaves for fuel and for thatching, and the fibres for making ropes. A date palm is either male or female, and dates grow only on the female trees. In spring the flowers of the male trees are picked and tied on to the female trees to pollinate their flowers. In some oases this is the occasion for a festival, and the men sing special songs to the trees. In autumn they climb the tall trunks again to gather the dates which grow at the top. These are taken to the market where the Bedouin buy their winter's supply.

The water which supplies the oases has often been under the ground for a very long time. Sometimes rainwater has been collecting in hollows in the rocks under the desert for thousands of years. In other places an underground river may be moving very very slowly — perhaps a kilometre in 40 years — through little cracks deep down in the rock. Nowadays engineers are trying to find these underground rivers and to sink wells to them, so as to bring the water to the surface. Desert soil is often fertile, so that if water can be brought to it, good crops can be grown. There is, however, the danger that water standing in pools or small canals in very hot lands attracts mosquitoes, which carry disease. In old days some oases in Arabia had to be abandoned because the people kept dying of fever. But if fish are put in the pools they will eat the mosquito larvae and so stop them spreading disease.

Oases are always in danger of getting buried in sand by sandstorms, and the people of oases have to fight a constant battle against the sand. Hedges of palm fronds are planted on the tops of the sand dunes to stop them sliding forwards, and sometimes rows of thick fir trees are planted round the gardens to stop the sand getting through. Nowadays the dunes are sometimes coated with oil to hold them firmly in one place, and then shrubs are planted along the top. But even with all these modern methods, life in an oasis is still a constant struggle against the desert.

6 LIFE IN A BEDOUIN TENT

ALI IS A Bedouin boy who lives in a tent in the desert. Each morning he and his father Mahmud fetch their camels, which have spent the night with one of their front legs tied up to prevent their wandering far from the tents. The Bedouin depend for their livelihood on their camels, the only animals which can live for days without water in the hot, bare desert. They ride their camels, use them to carry heavy loads, drink their milk, eat their meat, and use their hair to make tents. Mahmud and Ali love their camels and call each one by its own name. They think them very beautiful: in Arabic, the words for camel (*jamal*) and beautiful (*jamil*) are almost the same.

Ali and Mahmud drive the camels a long way to find the dry shrubs which only camels will eat. On the way they pass some footprints in the sand. 'These are made by three riding camels and a calf,' says Mahmud. 'Yes, and two men and a woman were walking beside them,' Ali replies, and looking carefully at the tracks, he adds, 'I think they passed 2 weeks ago.' 'Nearer 3 weeks ago,' says Mahmud, 'and these were camels of our cousins.' He shows Ali how to tell this from the footprints. By reading footprints in this way Bedouin can avoid their enemies in the desert and find their friends.

When they finally reach the shrubs, they find that almost all have been eaten. So Mahmud says, 'We must move camp tomorrow. Our chief says that there is pasture 2 days' journey to the north, where it rained 3 weeks ago.' Most of the year the Bedouin travel in the desert in search of pasture; only in the autumn do they come to an oasis to buy dates and grain and to sell their camels.

So Mahmud and Ali bring the camels back to the camp. At the wells a crowd of camels are pushing, stamping, and roaring impatiently, waiting for a drink. A few camels are pulling ropes attached to leather buckets, which are lowered in the wells and then pulled up and emptied into troughs, from which the animals drink. It is only when they can camp near a well that people and animals have enough to drink.

Behind the wells and sheltered from the wind by a ridge of hills stands a row of long, black tents. These belong to Ali's family — his grandfather, father, and uncles. Guard dogs welcome them as Mahmud and Ali reach their tent. Ali's sister Aisha has just come in from looking after the family's sheep all day, in a valley near the camp. In the women's part of the tent everything is tidy. The sleeping rugs are folded and piled in the middle of the tent, forming a wall between the women's and

men's parts. The sacks of grain, which must last the family until next year, are stacked in the tent, and also the black goat skins for carrying water, and one or two cooking pots. The men's part of the tent is almost as bare. Three brass coffee pots, a pan for roasting coffee, and some small cups are stacked in the middle near a little fireplace, round which heavy wooden camel saddles, covered with sheep skins, are arranged for guests to lean on. At the back of the tent a falcon sits on her perch, waiting for Mahmud to take her out to hunt hares or buzzards. These are all the family's possessions, for people who are always on the move cannot carry much with them. In the morning, when they move, the women will dismantle the heavy tent and load it on a camel's back; and when next they stop, the women will set the tent up again.

For supper Ali and Aisha have a bowl of camel's milk and some dry home-made bread. Although they usually have little to eat and are very thin, they are strong and healthy. Only when there is a visitor, do they eat really well. Then their father may kill a camel or sheep, and the meat is served on a mound of rice. The visitor is served first, then the father, and Aisha and her mother eat last.

When food is short the family try to avoid strangers who might stay for a meal; but if a stranger does come, they must kill an animal for him, even if it is their last one, for no Arab must fail in hospitality (see Chapter 8).

After supper the men drink coffee and talk. Often they talk of their relatives. Every Bedouin belongs to his family tribe, of which he is very proud. Ali knows all about his famous ancestors and the stories of the battles they fought. Sometimes the men talk of the old days when the Bedouin were not so poor or hungry because they could sell their camels well. Now townspeople buy cars, not camels. Also, in the old days, when there were no laws, the Bedouin could raid other tribes and steal their herds. Now the government has stopped Bedouin raids, and Land Rovers and aircraft reach all over the deserts to see that order is kept. Life is no longer so exciting; indeed it is getting more and more difficult for the Bedouin to survive.

7 THE ARAB FAMILY

'HOW LONELY ENGLISH children must be,' said an Arab boy, whose school had just received letters from English school children about life in their village. The Arab children were astonished that English children should live in such small families. They had written to the English children about their five or six brothers and sisters, their grandparents who lived with them, and the aunt, uncle, and cousins who lived in the same house too. Arabs think relatives very important, and any Arab child can always explain just what relation everyone in the village is to himself: 'She is the daughter of my mother's brother' (not at all the same as 'The daughter of my father's brother'), 'He is my grandfather's cousin', and so on. An Arab tribe is really a large family.

Most Arab children have many brothers and sisters. Arabs have some of the biggest families in the world, and they are proud of the number of children they have, especially of sons. They think sons much more important than daughters. An Arab mother, when asked how many children she had, replied 'Five'. 'Then who are all these other children?' 'Oh, they are all mine, but I only counted the boys, of course.' In old days desert Arabs sometimes even buried baby girls at birth because they only wanted boys, and they are still delighted when a boy is born, and disappointed if the baby is a girl.

Arab boy babies are often dressed like girls

Arab children have a very free life, doing what they like and often being spoilt by grown-ups. But when they become about 12, things change. All of a sudden everyone is very strict with them. In villages and small towns the girls still hardly go out of the house, and if they do go out, they must cover their faces with a veil. Teenagers are not expected to have fun, but help their mothers and fathers with their work; and they marry very young. The honour of the family depends on the girls' good behaviour. A girl may not talk to a boy, except her own brother, and if the neighbours see her doing so, she is disgraced. In fact in some parts of the Arab world, if a girl is thought to have behaved badly, her brother may kill her, and the neighbours will admire him for doing his duty. In such places a mother may not leave the house, even to take her child to the doctor, lest the neighbours might think she was not 'respectable'.

In the desert, where these rules of behaviour first grew up, it was, in fact, never possible for women to live quite apart from men. Though the tents had a curtain separating the men's part from

Children from all over the Arab World, some wearing traditional and some modern dress

the women's, men and women had to meet outside, and even work together. And today in the big cities people are giving up these strict rules and behaving more like people in cities all over the world. Women usually no longer wear a veil there, and even have jobs in shops and offices. Girls can meet friends, and even sometimes go out in the evenings. It is in the villages and countryside that the old rules are kept most strictly. In many villages there are no women to be seen in the streets at all.

In the past Arab boys and girls never chose whom they would marry. They married whom their father chose, and this might be someone they had never seen before, though if possible their father would choose his own niece or nephew. Now, in the cities at any rate, many young Arabs hope to have a choice, but it is still common for boys and girls to have to marry their cousins. An

Arab from Palestine tells this story of his own family: 'My father had to marry his cousin. He had no choice, and he barely knew her. I myself had seen my wife and wanted to marry her, but we could never speak to each other alone. Her mother or her brother were always with us. But my daughter went away to university. One day I received a telegram — "Dear daddy, I have got engaged; please send your blessing." At first I was shocked, but then I realized that the world is changing.'

As many Arabs have no choice of whom they marry, it is not surprising that some of them are not happy and want to change. Their religion allows a man to divorce his wife by saying 'I divorce you' three times. But it is very difficult, often impossible, for a woman to divorce her husband. The Arab religion, Islam, allows a man to have four wives at once, but few men have more than one wife at once nowadays. In the past a rich man kept a *harem*, the place where his wives, women, and slave girls lived. Some rich sheikhs are said to have had hundreds of women in their harems. But now men do not have harems in Arab countries, for life is growing more like life in Europe all the time.

8 ARAB HOSPITALITY

AS SOON AS a traveller crossing the lonely desert sees in the distance the long, low, black shapes of Bedouin tents (see Chapter 6), he knows he is safe for a night's shelter. Whether he is friend or foe, Arabs will always offer him hospitality for 3 days. This is the custom of the desert, which all Bedouin obey, for their life in the barren desert, as well as the traveller's, may one day depend on it. In fact many tribes have a special guest tent, and many villages a guest house.

A visitor is greeted with the words 'Ahlan wa sahlan', which means: 'you have come to your own people and your way is plain'. The visitor sits cross-legged on a rug on the floor and is offered a cup of coffee. Making coffee is a complicated ceremony which Arabs enjoy greatly. First they roast the green beans in a special pan over the fire; then they grind them in a pestle and mortar — or in towns they may now use a coffee grinder. Then the coffee, sugar, and water are cooked together in a long-spouted coffee pot, and are sometimes flavoured with the seeds of the spice plant cardamon. When it is ready, the coffee is poured into tiny cups without handles. It is good manners to drink several cups. When he has had enough the guest twists his cup round between his thumb and finger, which means 'No more, thank you'.

It is a point of honour to an Arab to feed his guest well. He will even kill his last animal to provide a good meal, and if he is expecting his visitor, a great feast is prepared. In the desert the meat is served on a huge, round, metal tray, which is placed on the ground in the middle of the circle of guests, who eat the food with their right hands, tearing off chunks of meat, and rolling the rice into little balls. Often the host does not eat with his guests, for he is too busy making sure that they eat as much as they possibly can. The polite guest keeps refusing more, while his host urges him to continue, offering him the tastiest morsels. The guest often has to eat far more than he really wants, in order to satisfy his host.

A Bedouin entertaining his guests

After the meal, bowls of water are brought round for the guests to wash their hands; and then they are served coffee, and sometimes also very sweet, sticky cakes and sweetmeats. Rich Arabs also often give splendid presents to their guests; indeed, a guest must be careful not to admire too warmly any of his host's things, for the hospitable host may offer them to him as a gift, and then it is rude to refuse.

It is not only in the desert that the Arabs are hospitable. A stranger walking along a village street will be invited into many homes for a cup of coffee or very sweet tea, sometimes made with mint, and if he wishes to stay the night, someone will always offer him a bed and meals. In the big cities this kind of hospitality is not so common, though it is still the custom for shopkeepers to offer coffee to their customers. A small boy is sent running to the nearest café or coffee seller, to return with a little tray laden with tiny cups of coffee.

Food is particularly important in the Arab world, perhaps because it is so difficult to produce that it cannot be taken for granted. So much of the Arab lands is desert, where no food grows, that the people of these countries never have as much food as they would like. So, apart from these occasional feasts, the desert people learn to live mainly on a little grain which they buy, on milk, yoghourt, and eggs which they get from their own animals, and dates which grow in the oases. They can very rarely afford to kill an animal for meat. So most desert Arabs are very thin, but they are tough and wiry for all that. The weak ones seldom live long. Of course, people in hot climates can keep healthy on much less food than people in cold climates.

Washing after the meal

A wooden milk bowl, a coffee grinder and cup, spoons, coffee pot, grapes, water melon, pomegranates, and dates

Even in the towns most Arabs eat little. They prepare bread in many different ways. In many places it is baked on hot ashes, making it crunchy on the outside, but also rather dusty. In other places the bread looks like a pancake, and is rolled around something tasty or dipped into cream cheese or creamed vegetables. In the mountains of Lebanon, these bread pancakes are enormous. A girl stretches the ball of dough by throwing it from one hand to the other and catching it over her arms. When it is very thin and about 60 centimetres across, she places it on top of a domed oven, where it quickly becomes crispy, and delicious.

The Arabs make some special dishes. *Kebabs* are little pieces of meat cooked on a skewer over a fire or grill. Small birds are cooked in the same way; the Lebanese go out shooting sparrows, robins, and thrushes, and the Bedouin catch small birds in little traps. In North Africa people make *couscous*, a pile of fine grain, served with a spicy stew of mutton and vegetables and lots of red pepper. In Lebanon, *mezze* consists of twenty or thirty little dishes of salads, meat, fish, vegetables, and cheese, cut into small chunks or creamed. The guests dip pieces of bread into each dish in turn and drink *arak*, a strange, white drink tasting of aniseed. Lebanese will happily while away a whole afternoon over their *mezze*.

23

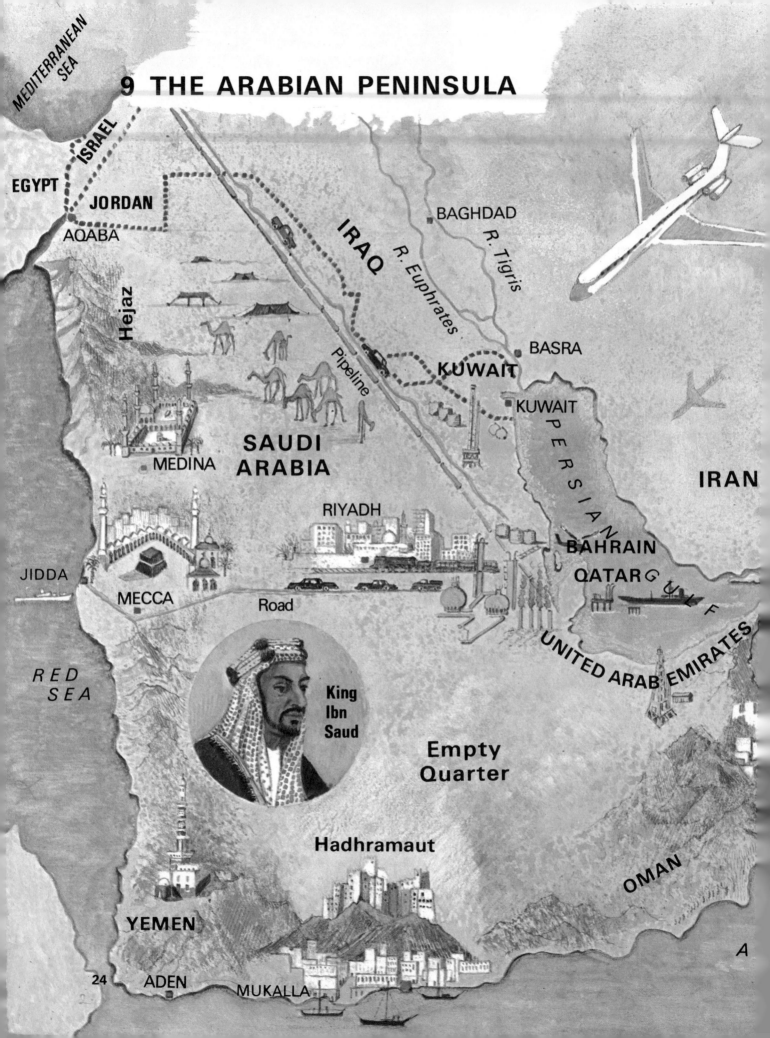

9 THE ARABIAN PENINSULA

MEDITERRANEAN SEA

ISRAEL

EGYPT

JORDAN

AQABA

Hejaz

IRAQ

BAGHDAD

R. Euphrates

R. Tigris

BASRA

KUWAIT

KUWAIT

SAUDI ARABIA

Pipeline

MEDINA

RIYADH

JIDDA

MECCA

Road

King Ibn Saud

RED SEA

P E R S I A N   G U L F

BAHRAIN

QATAR

IRAN

UNITED ARAB EMIRATES

Empty Quarter

Hadhramaut

OMAN

YEMEN

ADEN

MUKALLA

24

A

ARABIA WAS THE Arab's first home. Before the 7th century all Arabs lived in Arabia, and the lands where Arabs now live belonged to other peoples. In those days the Arabs were not a very important people, and there were not very many of them. They lived a hard life in a land which is mostly desert, and they were not able to have proper homes; they had to move about all the time to find food. Every now and then some of them left Arabia to try to make a better life in another land. Abraham and his people were one such nomad tribe. They settled in Mesopotamia, in what is now Iraq (see Chapter 21). Then, in the 7th century, very many Arabs began to leave the Arabian Peninsula and to sweep across all the lands which we now call the Arab world (see Chapter 12).

Most of Arabia today is still much as it was when the first Arabs lived there. Although Arabia is as big as western Europe, there are no more people there than there are in London, for in much of Arabia only Bedouin can live: only Bedouin know how to survive in so hot and barren a land (see Chapter 6). They could hardly manage to live in the desert were it not for their camels, which can travel hundreds of kilometres without water. With their camels the Bedouin can travel into the most distant deserts, while those Bedouin who keep sheep and goats have to stay nearer to the edge of the desert.

The Bedouin group together in tribes, which are like very large families (see Chapter 7). A tribe is ruled by a sheikh, and each tribe regards a part of the desert as being its land, and only its members can water their animals in the wells there. The Bedouin tribes used to be very powerful, and they used to make the people in the towns and oases pay them tribute, and the caravans of camels crossing the desert used to have to pay the Bedouin to protect them. Sometimes the tribes fought each other; and often they raided each other's herds, so if the herds of one tribe became large because there had been rain in their area, the other tribes soon stole enough of them to even out the numbers again.

At the beginning of this century the Bedouin still did as they liked in Arabia. Then, in 1902, a young Arab prince, called Abd al Aziz ibn Saud, whose family had been driven into exile, returned secretly to the town of his ancestors, Riyadh. He climbed over the mud walls one dark night and opened the gates to his friends, and by the morning he had captured the town. During the next 20 years he conquered nearly all Arabia, which was called Saudi Arabia after him, and he made Riyadh its capital. There remained a few small states around the edge of Arabia which were still ruled by their own princes, and the mountainous country of the Yemen in the south-west of Arabia also remained independent (see Chapter 41).

Ibn Saud was a very strict king. He forced the Bedouin to stop fighting and raiding and made them respect and fear him. He ruled his vast kingdom as though he were the sheikh of a tribe; anyone could come to him and he would listen to their complaints. A Bedouin might come to him as though he were a Bedouin sheikh and begin: 'Oh Abd al Aziz, my neighbour has taken my camels . . .' He was very strict about religion: there are special police wearing green turbans whose job it was, and still is, to see that people say their prayers and obey the religious rules.

Ibn Saud knew that Arabia must grow modern like the rest of the world, especially since it was discovered that there was a great deal of oil in Arabia. So he allowed an American oil company to dig oil wells there. As they found more and more oil under the sands, so Ibn Saud and the sheikhs ruling the little states round him grew richer and richer. The Arabs in the towns, and even some Bedouin, took jobs as oilmen and grew rich too. In the last 20 years big cities have grown up beside the old Arab towns, and huge modern buildings stand side by side with mud-walled houses. Today, there are dual carriageways and fast cars, while beside the modern roads camels and donkeys still plod along, carrying their loads to the cities. For Saudi Arabia is a strange mixture of the old and the new. About half the people of the Arabian Peninsula, in spite of the riches which oil has brought to their country, still live in tents in the desert, like Ali and Aisha (see Chapter 6), knowing little of the new ways in the towns. And women in Arabia still have little freedom. For instance, in Arabia only a man, not a woman, may drive one of the modern cars.

I A N

10 MUHAMMAD, THE PROPHET OF GOD

سُورَةُ فَاتِحَةِ الْكِتَابِ
بِسْمِ اللّٰهِ الرَّحْمٰنِ الرَّحِيمِ، الْحَمْدُ لِلّٰهِ رَبِّ الْعَالَمِينَ، الرَّحْمٰنِ الرَّحِيمِ،
مَالِكِ يَوْمِ الدِّينِ، إِيَّاكَ نَعْبُدُ وَإِيَّاكَ نَسْتَعِينُ،
إِهْدِنَا الصِّرَاطَ الْمُسْتَقِيمَ، صِرَاطَ الَّذِينَ أَنْعَمْتَ عَلَيْهِمْ
غَيْرِ الْمَغْضُوبِ عَلَيْهِمْ وَلَا الضَّالِّينَ

The first lines of the Koran in Arabic writing

MECCA AND MEDINA are the holy cities of the Arabs, about 320 kilometres apart in the mountainous desert of Saudi Arabia, near the Red Sea. In ancient times people used to make pilgrimages to Mecca to worship a strange black stone, called the Ka'ba, which they believed to be holy.

In 570 a boy was born in Mecca who was named Muhammad (which is often written Mohammed). His father died before he was born, and his mother died when he was only 6. For a while the little boy lived with a Bedouin tribe. From them he learnt to speak beautiful Arabic, for the people of the desert spoke much better Arabic than the people of the towns. Later Muhammad lived with his grandfather, and then with his uncle.

Muhammad's uncle was a merchant. He sent caravans of camels into Syria and the Yemen. Muhammad probably travelled with his uncle's caravans, and then with the caravans of a rich widow called Khadija. He worked so well that she put him in charge of her business, and when he was 25 he married her. Though she was 15 years older than he was, they were very happy and had six children. As long as she lived he did not marry any other wives, although most Arabs in those days had several wives.

Muhammad used to go to a cave in a mountain nearby to think and pray. One day, when he was 40 years old, he suddenly heard a powerful voice speaking to him in the cave. It seemed to him that the Archangel Gabriel seized him by the throat and forced him to repeat a message that there was only one God. Muhammad went home feeling very worried. He told Khadija what had happened and said he did not want to go out and preach. He knew that the Christians and Jews believed there was only one God, but he was not sure this was true, nor that it was indeed God who had spoken to him. But he kept getting more messages, and he began to tell his friends about them. Afterwards these messages were remembered and were collected into a book called the *Koran*, which is the Muslims' Bible, for they believe that God himself gave them to Muhammad. Some messages told of the Jewish prophets, Abraham, Moses, and also of Jesus; some gave instructions for the way Muslims should live; some told about God. They were written in very beautiful Arabic.

Khadija was the first person to believe Muhammad, but gradually more and more people believed him. But some people in Mecca were frightened at his teaching, for they depended for their living on trade and on people coming on pilgrimage to the Ka'ba. They were afraid that Muhammad's preaching might put an end to the pilgrimage. Then both Khadija and Muhammad's uncle died in the same year, and Muhammad had no one to protect him. His enemies became more dangerous, and at last he and his followers fled to a small oasis town, 320 kilometres away — a town which became known as Medina, meaning 'The City', short for 'City of the Prophet'.

Muhammad fled to Medina in 622, and Muslims count their years from that date, instead of from the birth of Christ, as Christians do. When Muhammad arrived, the people of Medina were quarrelling among themselves. They asked him to be their judge and lawgiver, and soon he established peace in the town. The people of Medina became his followers, the first Muslims (or Moslems). Under Muhammad's leadership the people of Medina became strong, and they began to raid the caravans from Mecca. There were constant skirmishes between the two towns until, 2 years after Muhammad's escape, a big battle was fought between them. Mecca had more soldiers, but Medina won because Muhammad was such a clever commander.

Muhammad fought two more battles against Mecca, and then the two towns made peace. In order to achieve peace, Muhammad included the pilgrimage to Mecca (see Chapter 28) in his religion of Islam. Muhammad gradually brought more and more Bedouin tribes under his control and converted them to Islam, and he made strong alliances all over Arabia. He was so strong that, when the people of Mecca broke the truce with him, he forced them to surrender straight away. He removed all the idols from the temple round the Ka'ba and made it into a mosque for Muslims. He treated the people kindly, and soon most of them became Muslims too.

Muhammad taught the people of the whole region to live in peace and brotherhood. He preached about God, and gave his people rules for

their daily lives. He ordered that no man might have more than four wives at once and that he must treat them fairly. He himself had several more wives after Khadija died; his favourite wife was Aisha, whom he married when she was a little girl of about 10.

In 632 Muhammad fell ill. He preached a farewell sermon to his people, urging them to stay together; he repeated that there was only one God, and that his followers must live as brothers and not fight each other. Then he returned to Medina, where he died in the house of Aisha.

After Muhammad's death, his father-in-law, Abu Bakr, spoke to the people saying: 'Whoever worships Muhammad, let him know that Muhammad is dead; but whoever worships God, let him know that God lives and does not die.' Muhammad had taught his people to believe in one God. After his death, his religion lived and spread half across the world.

The voice of Allah speaking to Muhammad from the cave

11 ISLAM

NO ONE CAN travel in the Arab world without being aware of the Arabs' religion. One may see an Arab spread a mat in a quiet corner of the street or in a field, take off his shoes, kneel down, touch his forehead to the ground, and then murmur his prayers. All Arabs face in the same direction when they pray — towards Mecca, their holy city. In any Arab town or village there is a mosque, the Muslims' church, and from the tower of the mosque a man calls all Arabs to prayer several times a day. The first call is at daybreak. In the desert at these appointed times, the Bedouin gets off his camel and kneels in the sand; in the fields the peasants stop work and pray where they are. Outside a mosque is a fountain so that people may wash before entering the mosque. Also everyone takes off his shoes when he goes into the mosque. In the towns all the shops are shut on Fridays, for Friday is the Muslim day of rest and prayer. On Fridays especially there are usually beggars in the streets, for Muslims must give alms to beggars.

The evening call to prayer

The religion which Muhammad first gave to the Arabs in Arabia in the 7th century is called Islam, which means 'submission to God'. The Arabic name for God is Allah. Now this religion has spread wherever Arabs have gone and far further still — for example to Turkey, Persia, Pakistan, and Indonesia. It is the second largest religion in the world. The most important thing which Muhammad taught his followers was that there is only one God — not many, as most Arabs had believed before. Belief in one God was not a new idea in the Middle East. The Jews, a wandering tribe of herdsmen, had been declaring for centuries that there was only one God. They called Him Jehovah, and wrote their ideas about Him in the books of the Old Testament. Then Jesus Christ, a Jew of Palestine, preached new things about God, which are written in the New Testament, and today about one-third of all the people in the world are Christians.

Muhammad taught that Allah was the same God that the Jews and Christians worshipped. He taught in the Muslim holy book, the Koran, a new way of worshipping God, a way suited to his people. So Jews, Christians, and Muslims all worship the same God, and they all respect the same ancestors and prophets: Adam, Abraham, Moses, and others. (To a Muslim Jesus is the last of the great prophets before Muhammad.) Each religion keeps one day as holy: the Jews keep Saturday as their 'Sabbath'; the Christians keep Sunday, and the Muslims, Friday. All three religions think of Jerusalem as a particularly holy city, and this has led to many wars between them.

The religion of Islam is based on the Koran, which Muslims believe Allah Himself dictated to Muhammad. Arabs always keep their Koran on the top shelf of their bookcase — above other books. Islam lays down five special rules for Muslims. The first is that there is no other god but Allah — in Arabic *La Allah illa Allah* — and that Muhammad is His prophet. The second is prayer, at five special times each day. A Muslim can pray anywhere, but he must face in the direction of Mecca. Muslims are called to prayer by a man

Alms for the love of Allah

called a *muezzin* from the tower, or minaret, of the mosque, often now with loudspeakers.

The third rule is to give alms to the poor: a Muslim should give away about one tenth of his money, for charity is considered an important virtue. The fourth rule is to keep Ramadan, which is like a very strict Lent. It lasts for one month, and during this month a Muslim may neither eat nor drink from sunrise to sunset, however hot it is. At the end of the month, when the new moon is first seen, there is a great feast. Every family, if they can, kills a sheep, and there are bonfires and flags and parties. The fifth rule is that every Muslim, if he can possibly afford it, should make a pilgrimage to Mecca once in his lifetime (see Chapter 28).

Islam has many other rules about how people should live their lives, that they may not drink alcohol, for example, nor gamble, nor lend money for profit. Some of these, especially those concerned with women, seem very old-fashioned today, but when Muhammad introduced them, about 1,300 years ago, they made great improvements in the way people lived. Until very recently they have hardly been changed at all, and even today they are the rules which control family life in many parts of the Arab world.

12 THE ARAB CONQUESTS

WHEN MUHAMMAD DIED in Medina in 632, the religion he had founded still existed only in Arabia. By 732, 100 years later, Islam had spread right across North Africa and into Spain and all over the countries of the Middle East. The Arabs, a quite small group of desert tribes, had conquered all these countries. The Arab World in a 100 years spread from the Arabian Peninsula to include all the countries shown on the map on p. 8. How did such extraordinary conquests take place?

A great difference between the Founder of the Christian religion, Jesus of Nazareth, and Muhammad, the founder of Islam, is that Jesus was purely a religious leader and would take no part in political movements, while Muhammad was a political leader as well as a religious one (see Chapter 10). He taught that all Muslims should be brothers and live in peace with each other; but his followers were warlike Arab tribes and believed that Islam should be carried all over the world by the sword. For example, the great Arab leader Khalid ibn al Walid was nicknamed 'the Sword of God'. With-

in 2 years of Muhammad's death Khalid had led an Arab army across the waterless desert to conquer Iraq and Syria. All Arab soldiers believed that it was their duty as good Muslims to fight 'the Holy War', and that if they did so they were certain of salvation.

The Arab armies always fought across deserts for they felt at home in the open desert. Wherever they advanced, they liked to have desert behind them, to which they could retreat if they were in trouble, and where the enemy would be afraid to pursue them. Another reason why the Arab armies were so successful was that the countries round them had exhausted themselves in fighting with each other, and so could not put up any strong defence against the invaders.

The Arab armies usually built great armed camps on the edge of the desert in the countries they conquered, and ruled the new lands from there. But they took as wives the women of the conquered countries. According to Muhammad's rules, a Muslim might have four wives. So soon they had large families to rule the countries they had conquered, or to go on to conquer new lands.

When Muhammad died in 632, his two closest friends, Abu Bakr and Umar, became the leaders of the Muslims. Both of these men were the fathers of wives of Muhammad. At first Abu Bakr became Caliph (that is, Successor to the Prophet), and when, 2 years later, he died, Umar became Caliph. Although he was soon the ruler of a great empire and very rich, the Caliph Umar always kept to the simple life Muhammad had preached. When he rode into Jerusalem, which his armies had conquered, he rode on a camel, wearing a coarse woollen shirt and cloak, and with only one attendant. He found his commanders wearing gorgeous silk gowns and he was furious with them. If he thought his commanders were becoming too powerful, he took away their command and the riches they had captured. But he was not harsh to other religions and insisted that the Church of the Holy Sepulchre in Jerusalem should remain a Christian Church.

As the Arab world grew larger, it became more and more difficult for one Caliph to rule it all from Medina, his capital in Arabia, and rebellions broke out. The Caliph who succeeded Umar was murdered, and his successor Ali, a cousin of Muhammad's and husband of his daughter Fatima, had to spend 5 years in fighting rebellious Muslims who would not accept him as Caliph. Then he also was murdered.

This was the beginning of a split in the Arab world. Ali's followers became known as Shi'ite Muslims and spread in Iraq and Persia, and the leader of his enemies, the Sunni Muslims, became Caliph with his capital at Damascus. Muslims are still divided into Shi'ites and Sunnis, much as Christians are into Catholics and Protestants.

The Caliph Omar rides into Jerusalem

31

13 THE ARABIAN NIGHTS

ONCE UPON A TIME an eastern king called Shahriyar had a very beautiful wife. One day, when he came home from hunting, he found his wife in the arms of a Negro slave with whom she had fallen in love. Shahriyar was so furious that he killed them both. Determined that no wife of his should ever betray him again, he decided to marry a different young girl each evening and have her put to death the next morning.

It was the duty of his vizier (or chief minister) to find a girl each day for the king to marry. Before long there were hardly any girls left, and every family was weeping for its lost daughters. Now the vizier himself had two beautiful daughters. The elder, called Sheherazade, was clever as well as beautiful. She asked her father to let her marry the king as she had thought of a plan which might prevent his putting any more girls to death. The vizier was very sad, for he was sure that he would lose his daughter. But he had to find a bride for the king that night, or he would lose his own head.

That night, Sheherazade begged the king that her sister might visit her to say goodbye. Her sister asked Sheherazade to tell them one last story to pass the long hours of the night. Sheherazade began to tell an exciting story, but just as she came to the most exciting part, she stopped because it was morning. Shahriyar so longed to hear the rest of the story that he decided to let her live till the next night. The next night the same thing happened; at daybreak Sheherazade was again at a very exciting point in the story. Once again she was allowed to live. For one thousand and one nights Sheherazade continued to tell the king stories, always stopping at the exciting point. By that time Shahriyar loved Sheherazade much too much to think of putting her to death, and they had had several children.

The stories which Sheherazade told Shahriyar are called the *Arabian Nights*. They include many well-known stories such as Ali Baba and the Forty Thieves, Aladdin, and Sinbad the Sailor. The stories were first collected together in Baghdad about 1,000 years ago. Some of the oldest stories come from India and the East; others came from Persia, and many tell of Baghdad — a fabulous, fairy-tale city. In fact, life in Baghdad could have been like that 1,000 years or more ago. Rich people in Baghdad at that time lived in luxurious palaces, with fountains playing in the courtyards, and held great banquets where hundreds of slaves waited on the guests and dancing slave girls entertained them. In Baghdad one Caliph actually owned 11,000 slaves, and another had 4,000 slave girls. Baghdad (see Chapter 14) was the capital of the great Arab empire; prisoners captured in war were brought back as slaves, and wealth filled the treasure houses of the city.

There are descriptions of treasures and jewels in almost every story of the *Arabian Nights*. Sinbad invites a poor porter into his mansion and serves him a banquet on gold and silver plates; Ali Baba finds the robbers' cave piled high with jewels and gold coins; Aladdin goes down into an amazing garden under the ground where the trees bear fruits made of diamonds, emeralds, rubies, and pearls. The story-teller really might have seen such sights in Baghdad in olden days. The wife of the great Caliph, Harun al Rashid, who was ruling in the year 800, always wore shoes studded with jewels, and would only have gold and silver dishes on her table. Another Caliph wore golden armour and rode on a saddle of gold, and a later Caliph, who wanted to impress messengers coming from a foreign king, had them met by a procession of slaves leading a hundred lions. He received them in a palace decorated with golden curtains, and a great tree made of gold and silver, on whose branches perched gold and silver birds, which chirped mechanically. When in 1258 the Mongols captured Baghdad (see Chapter 19), their leader piled the Caliph's treasure round his tent in great glittering mounds.

The people in the *Arabian Nights* stories often make long journeys round the world. Sometimes, of course, they just rub a magic ring or lamp and a genie whisks them off to Morocco or China. But Sinbad sets off in a sailing boat to visit the lands of the East; and another traveller goes to Cairo from Baghdad by camel, and has to walk most of the way home! In fact, Arabs often did take long journeys: merchant ships frequently sailed down the river from Baghdad on trading voyages to the East; camel caravans set off across the desert to the West; scholars travelled far and wide across the Arab world, exchanging knowledge and bringing new ideas and new stories. Many of Sinbad's adventures are based on the real experiences of Baghdad merchants who could not help exaggerating their adventures a little when eventually they reached home.

14 DAMASCUS AND BAGHDAD

THE FABULOUS CITIES of the *Arabian Nights*, Damascus and Baghdad, were each in turn capital of the Arab empire and the greatest cities of their time. Their streets were paved and well lit, with beautiful buildings and splendid palaces, at a time when European towns were mostly poor, dark, and muddy. They bustled with wealthy merchants and rich courtiers in magnificent robes. Visitors could scarcely believe their eyes before such wealth and beauty (see map p. 9).

Today Damascus is the capital of Syria, and Baghdad is the capital of Iraq; but neither city is any longer splendid. They are dusty, rather dingy towns with some beautiful buildings, but mostly a mixture of poor old houses and rather ugly modern buildings. This is because both cities were destroyed by the Mongols hundreds of years ago, and now they are no longer rich and powerful.

Damascus is one of the oldest cities in the world, and is often mentioned in the Old Testament. It was important long before the Arabs captured it in 635. It is built at the foot of a bleak mountain range, where a clear, cold river flows out of the hills. The river divides into many little streams which flow through the streets and gardens and keep the city fresh in summer. The houses cluster along the streams, or cling to the steep sides of the mountain.

When the Arabs captured it, they were so delighted with the fresh water and green gardens, where all kinds of fruits grew and birds sang, that they made it their capital. But they were still desert people at heart, so the Arab rulers built palaces far out in the desert, to which they would go, with their falcons and huntings dogs, to hunt game as their Bedouin ancestors had done.

The Arab Caliph in the 8th century wanted to build the most magnificent mosque in the world in Damascus; so he employed Christian workmen to make green and gold mosaic pictures all over the walls and to cover the pillars with sheets of gold. He had rich carpets spread on the floor. He did not mind how much it all cost. 'We have spent this money for God,' he said, 'and we will make no account of it.' The mosque still stands today, surrounded by an ancient Roman wall and by the old markets; but its treasures have long ago been destroyed or stolen.

34

The Great Mosque in Damascus

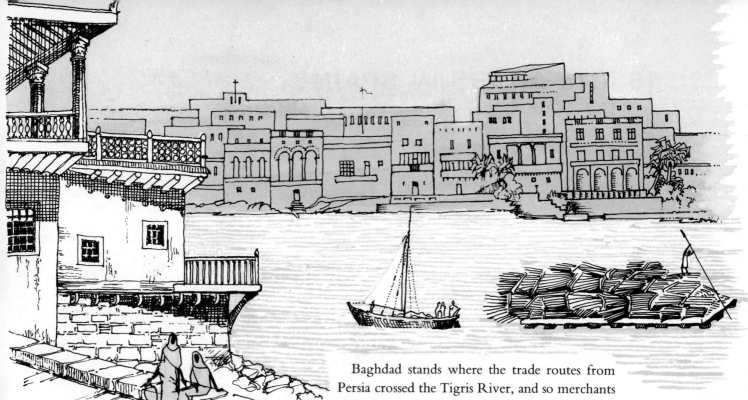

Damascus was a strongly fortified town, surrounded by high walls. In the 11th century, when the Crusaders (see Chapter 17) tried to capture it, they failed. The leader of the Muslims against the Crusaders, Saladin (see Chapter 18), made Damascus his headquarters and was buried there. Christians like to visit it because St. Paul was converted on his way there, and was taken to a house in the Street Called Straight, which still exists. It is part of the old markets where fine brocades and damask cloths are still sold; nearby are gold markets, carpet markets, and stalls of spices and candied fruits. But Damascus is not the important city that it was when the whole Arab world was ruled from there.

In the 8th century a Caliph of Damascus decided to build a new capital for himself further east, on the banks of the Tigris River; he called his city Baghdad. He built a circular citadel, surrounded by a double wall, inside which only he might ride on horseback; everyone else had to walk. Inside the citadel he built a magnificent palace, hung with carpets and curtains and cooled by gleaming marble and fountains splashing in shady courtyards.

Baghdad stands where the trade routes from Persia crossed the Tigris River, and so merchants and scholars from Persia and the countries further east came to the city, bringing new ideas with them. From these scholars the Arabs learnt the numbers which we use today, how to make paper, and many other things not known in Europe. They founded a great university in Baghdad where books from Persia, and India, and also from Greece, were translated into Arabic. Baghdad became such a centre of learning that scholars from many different countries came there to study and wrote important books in Arabic. Merchant ships sailed up the Tigris on trading expeditions to buy silks, jewels, and spices from the east, Negro slaves from Africa, and furs and honey from the north. Baghdad became one of the richest cities in the world.

After about 200 years, the Caliphs of Baghdad grew weaker and were unable to protect their city against enemies from outside. Then in the 13th century the fierce Mongol tribes from the east descended on the city and destroyed it (see Chapter 19). It never recovered its old greatness and beauty, though today it is growing quickly again. In modern Baghdad, the capital of Iraq, there are big new buildings as well as tin shacks and mud houses, and busy traffic swirls along the wide roads. But nothing is left of the fabulous city of the *Arabian Nights*.

15 THE ARABS IN SPAIN

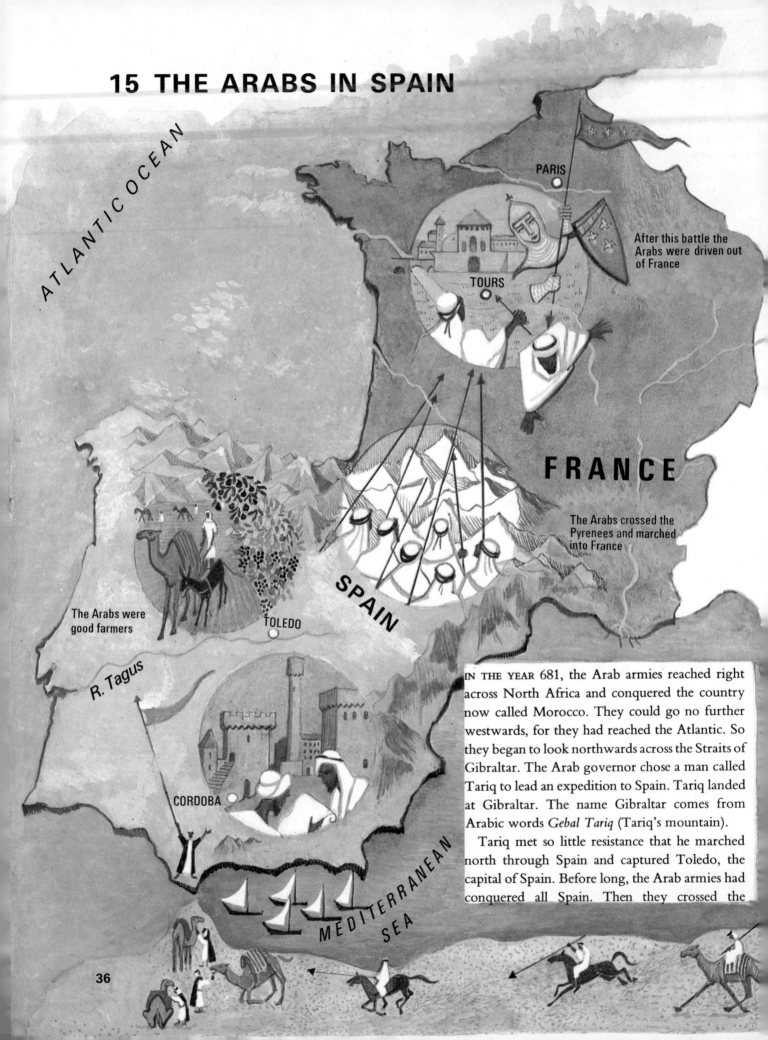

ATLANTIC OCEAN

PARIS

After this battle the
Arabs were driven out
of France

TOURS

FRANCE

The Arabs crossed the
Pyrenees and marched
into France

SPAIN

The Arabs were
good farmers

TOLEDO

R. Tagus

CORDOBA

MEDITERRANEAN SEA

IN THE YEAR 681, the Arab armies reached right across North Africa and conquered the country now called Morocco. They could go no further westwards, for they had reached the Atlantic. So they began to look northwards across the Straits of Gibraltar. The Arab governor chose a man called Tariq to lead an expedition to Spain. Tariq landed at Gibraltar. The name Gibraltar comes from Arabic words *Gebal Tariq* (Tariq's mountain).

Tariq met so little resistance that he marched north through Spain and captured Toledo, the capital of Spain. Before long, the Arab armies had conquered all Spain. Then they crossed the

Pyrenees Mountains and marched into France. It looked as though they were going to conquer all Europe, as they had conquered North Africa and the Middle East. They had nearly reached Paris when they were at last stopped by the French king, Charles the Hammer, who defeated them in a desperate battle at Tours in the year 732, just 100 years after the death of Muhammad. Charles drove them right out of France, but they stayed in Spain for nearly 800 more years.

About 20 years later, a young Arab prince called Abd al Rahman, managed to escape from his enemies in Baghdad and make his way across North Africa to Spain. His family, who had ruled in Damascus for 100 years, had been invited to a feast, and there they were all murdered. Only Abd al Rahman was left alive, and he managed to escape. He dived into the River Euphrates, swam to the other side, and got away. For 5 years he wandered as a fugitive, poor and hungry, and often in disguise. But this tall, thin, red-headed young prince was brave and determined, and at last he managed to reach Spain. There, many Arabs remembered that he was the son of a great family, and they accepted him as their ruler. He soon captured Cordoba, the Arab capital in Spain.

The Caliph in Baghdad was furious that this young prince had escaped him, and he sent a new Governor to Spain. But Abd al Rahman soon defeated him. He cut off his head, wrapped it in one of the Caliph's black banners, and sent it to the Caliph at Baghdad. The Caliph said, 'Thanks be to Allah for having placed the sea between me and such an enemy!' and made no more attempt to interfere with Abd al Rahman. Nevertheless the young prince had to fight for many years to make his throne in Spain secure.

When at last he had overcome his enemies, Abd al Rahman set to work to make Cordoba and other Spanish cities as grand and beautiful as Damascus and Baghdad. He started to build the great mosque at Cordoba, which today is used as a Christian cathedral. It is a splendid building with over 1,000 columns, looking like a forest of fine marble and coloured stone.

After Abd al Rahman died his family continued to rule in Spain, and for the next 200 years the Arab kingdom in Spain was famous all over Europe for its prosperity and learning. The Arabs developed fine farms and gardens and worked out ways of bringing water to them. They grew grapes, olives and vegetables, as well as lovely flowers. Their city streets were paved and clean, and lit at night, unlike other cities in Europe. They had better architects and doctors — and even dressmakers and singers — than anywhere else in Europe. The first paper factories in Europe were set up in Spain, and the Arab craftsmen wove wool and silk, made fine leather and metal goods and beautiful jewellery, and also glass, pottery, and tiles. All these things were sold to other countries, and the kingdom of Cordoba became richer and richer.

In particular, the University at Cordoba became as famous a centre of learning as the University in Baghdad. A great ruler in the 10th century, Abd al Rahman III, spent much money on the University. He was the first to pay university teachers, and he gave grants to students from other countries; so all the best teachers and students came to Cordoba. Scholars studied mathematics, chemistry, astronomy, and medicine, and also geography, history and literature. They wrote many books, and the seventy great libraries contained thousands of books, all of which, in the days before printing, had to be written by hand. In fact, for several hundred years it was the Arabs, especially in Baghdad and Cordoba, who were the leaders of the world.

Not long after the death of Abd al Rahman III, the Arabs began quarrelling with each other and splitting into small states. The Christian states in northern Spain grew stronger and attacked the Arab states. For a long time the Arab kingdom of Granada remained powerful; but finally, in 1492, the Arabs were driven right out of Spain.

Baghdad

37

16 CAMEL CARAVANS

LONG BEFORE TRAINS or convoys of lorries were thought of, Arabs used to carry their goods across the desert on camel back, in what are called camel caravans. Encouraged by the songs of their drivers, a line of camels, as far as the eye could see, would plod one after the other along a desert track, their loads swaying as they walked.

An Arab merchant who joined such a caravan knew that he would have to spend weeks, perhaps months, jogging slowly across desert tracks beneath the fierce glare of the sun. The caravan would set off before dawn in order to cover as much ground as possible before the sun reached its full heat. Then they would stop and build little camp-fires to brew coffee and make porridge of crushed grain to eat with a few dates for breakfast. Then on they would go again for hours without break, walking over the hot sand — only a few lucky ones could ride — until finally the whole caravan stopped and collected together for a light supper. They would have travelled for about 10 hours and have covered 48 kilometres in the day. At nightfall they would make their camp. If all was safe and there were any desert plants to be found, they would let their camels loose to feed. But if they feared there were any raiders about, they would make the camels lie in a great circle,

and the men would sleep in the middle, among their goods. Again, the lucky ones might have a tent, but most would sleep in the open air. Guards posted round the circle would keep watch all night in case any raiders might try to steal the valuable merchandise. In the desert everyone must look after his own goods: there are no police.

Sometimes a caravan might consist of up to 3,000 camels and hundreds of merchants, all travelling together for safety. They would wait at the start of the caravan route until there were enough of them to hire a leader to control the party, guides to find the way, and guards to protect them. A caravan which was delayed or lost its way, even for a short time, might run out of water, which must all be carried in goat-skin bags on the backs of camels, and then everyone would die of thirst.

Caravan routes crossed the Sahara from the Mediterranean coast to Timbuktu, linking the lands of the West African Negroes, rich in ivory and salt and slaves, with the Arab lands of North Africa, and hence with Spain and Europe. Until the Europeans had discovered the sea passage around South Africa in 1488 (see Book 2), most of the trade with India, China, and the East came across the Arabian Desert. Few people dared travel by ship in the Red Sea or Persian Gulf because of the pirates (see Chapter 21).

In southern Arabia spices, coffee, gold, and frankincense were produced in the mountains.

These and the silks, spices, and precious stones brought across the sea from lands further east, were loaded onto camels in south-eastern Arabia to make the long journey up the coast, through Mecca and Medina, to the hills of Jordan (see map p. 9). There was only one place between central Arabia and Damascus where there was, and still is, plenty of fresh water. This is in Jordan, where Moses is said to have struck a rock with his staff and water gushed out to save the Israelites from dying of thirst in the Wilderness. A strange caravan city called Petra was built here in ancient times. It stood in a valley in the centre of steep cliffs of red rock, and was reached by a narrow gorge through the rock. The caravans from Arabia stopped at Petra to get water and fresh camels before going on northwards to Damascus or westwards to Egypt. The people of Petra made them pay heavily for this help, and so they became rich and were able to carve beautiful buildings in their red cliffs. We can still see Petra today, but no one lives there now.

Another caravan route followed the north coast of Arabia and along the Euphrates River. Then it turned westwards across the Syrian Desert, to Damascus and the Mediterranean coast, or southwards to Petra and Egypt. In the middle of the Syrian Desert was an oasis where the ancient caravan town of Palmyra was built, and between Palmyra and the Euphrates wells were dug, a

day's journey apart. So this caravan journey was comparatively easy, and caravans streamed into the great caravanserai at Palmyra, where they stopped to unload, and often to rest for a few days. Palmyra grew large and rich, until in 272 its queen, Zenobia, rebelled against the Romans, who destroyed the town. Now it is nothing but a desert village. There were other caravanserais, or *khans* as they are called, in northern Syria, with fine courtyards, store rooms, and bedrooms for the merchants. But all are empty and silent now.

Camel caravans became less important in the 15th century when the sea route around Africa was discovered, and again after 1869 when the Suez Canal was dug. The pirates were swept from the seas, and ships took the place of camels. Nowadays goods are taken across the deserts by lorry, and convoys of lorries bump across the rough caravan tracks. Small strings of camels still plod along towards an oasis, but merchants today find lorries more comfortable and far quicker.

17 THE CRUSADES

JUST AS ALL Muslims wanted to make a pilgrimage to Mecca, where Muhammad was born, so did Christian pilgrims want to go to the Holy Land where Jesus had lived — especially to Jerusalem. For a long time the Holy Land was ruled by a Christian Emperor from Constantinople, and so Christians could travel there safely. Even after the Arabs conquered Palestine, the Muslim rulers usually allowed Christian pilgrims to travel there freely. But in the 11th century a new danger arose.

Tribes of Turks had been gradually moving westwards from the borders of China, and when they reached the Arab lands in the 11th century, they began to settle there and were converted to the Muslim religion of Islam. The Caliphs of Baghdad were very weak at that time, and they welcomed the Turks, who soon became the rulers of Baghdad. Tribes of Turks captured many of the Arab cities, and for a while they even captured Jerusalem. They also invaded the lands of the

In 1095 Pope Urban called on all Christians to take up their crosses and go to rescue the Holy Land. Those who went were given crosses as a sign that they were fighting a holy war, and they were called Crusaders. Just as the Muslims had believed that the Arab armies carrying Islam to other countries were fighting a holy war, so did the Crusaders feel that they were fighting for God.

Thousands of Crusaders set out from France and Germany for the Holy Land. Some were led by knights in armour on horseback, their banners flying bravely; others were just ragged mobs, following a monk or priest, without arms or discipline, and stealing their food as they went. They passed Constantinople and were amazed by its splendour, for they were used to the rough life of Europe. Then they crossed the land that is now Turkey, where many died of hunger or heat, until they came to the fortified city of Antioch. It took the Crusaders 9 months to capture Antioch.

Christian Emperor of Constantinople, and everywhere at this time there was fighting and trouble. Christian pilgrims to Jerusalem found the roads too dangerous to travel along, and the Turks often attacked and ill-treated them. So the Emperor of Constantinople asked the Christians of Europe to help drive the Turks out of his lands, and to rescue the holy places from them.

Then some of the Crusaders, who were really more interested in winning land for themselves than in freeing Jerusalem, began to break away from the main army and make themselves rulers of neighbouring towns. The rest marched on.

Jerusalém was one of the strongest cities of the day, perched on a hilltop, with massive walls and towers. The Crusaders built wooden towers to place against the walls, and daring French knights jumped across from the top of them and climbed down into the town. After a fierce battle they captured the city. Then they killed everyone in it, Muslims and Jews, men, women, and children alike, until the streets were filled with dead.

The Crusaders were triumphant; they had already conquered Jerusalem and most of the coastline of Syria, Lebanon, and Palestine. But they had succeeded only because the Muslims (or Saracens as they called them) were always fighting each other and had no strong leader. The Crusaders built huge castles, or captured and strengthened Arab castles, to defend their lands. These castles were so strong that, in spite of all the battles, many are still standing. But the Crusaders were never able to unite for long under one leader, and their castles were often ruled by the sons of fathers who had been killed in battle. All the same, the Crusader kingdom of Jerusalem lasted for nearly 100 years, until a great Muslim leader called Saladin arose (see Chapter 18). He united the Arabs against the Crusaders and recaptured Jerusalem in 1187.

Immediately the German Emperor, the King of France, and Richard the Lion Heart of England led another Crusade to rescue the Holy City. Only Richard achieved anything; he was a splendid general, who defeated Saladin's army on one occasion and won back some cities. But he failed to recapture Jerusalem. Although the Crusaders stayed along the coasts of the Arab countries for 100 years more, they never recaptured Jerusalem.

In 1212 people had the idea that the Holy Land could be taken from the Muslims only by the young and innocent. And so 30,000 French children led by a shepherd boy called Stephen and 20,000 German children led by a boy called Nicholas set out to rescue the Holy Sepulchre. What happened to them we do not know, except that they never reached the Holy Land. They all disappeared — drowned at sea or killed by enemies or kidnapped by slave-traders.

There were other Crusades, too, but none of them had much success. When the Crusaders were finally driven out of the Arab lands, the Christians who had always lived there were driven out too, and had to seek refuge in the mountains of Lebanon, where many still live.

Crusader army attacking Jerusalem

41

18 SALADIN

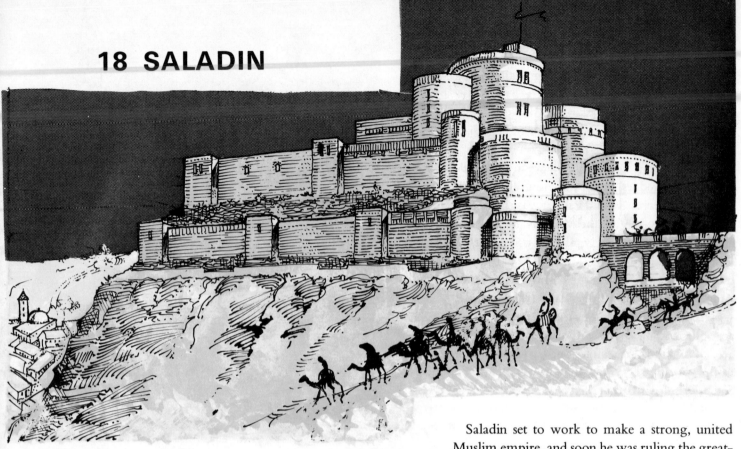

Kerak Castle

THE GREAT MUSLIM leader, Saladin, was not an Arab, but came from people called Kurds in the mountains in the north of Iraq. He was born in a town high up on the River Tigris. When he was a young man he joined the Syrian army, and he went with his uncle on a campaign to Egypt. Saladin did not really want to be a soldier, for he liked reading better than fighting, but in those days to be a soldier was thought the right thing for a young man.

Saladin helped his uncle win control of the country, and when his uncle died, he became ruler of Egypt. The Egyptians soon learnt that this slight, solemn-looking young man was a strong ruler. He put down revolts very firmly and severely; but he was generous to those who did not oppose his rule.

After Saladin had been in Egypt for 10 years, the ruler of Syria died, and the people of Damascus, who needed a strong ruler to oppose the Crusaders, asked Saladin to become Sultan of Syria as well as ruler of Egypt.

Saladin set to work to make a strong, united Muslim empire, and soon he was ruling the greatest Arab empire which had existed for 200 years. As he grew stronger he grew more merciful and generous. Unlike many other commanders of his time, he did not enjoy killing people, and Arabs and Crusaders alike were amazed to have their lives spared, when they themselves would certainly have taken Saladin's life if they had had the chance. Saladin also always kept his promises, which few people in those days thought at all necessary. He made good strong laws and treated everyone in his empire with justice. Also he built roads and canals and encouraged trade.

Saladin's most hated enemy was the Crusader Reynald, ruler of one of the strongest Crusader castles, Kerak. Every time a truce was signed between the Crusaders and Muslims, and peaceful trade between the two peoples began to grow, Reynald would break the truce and attack merchant or pilgrim caravans on their way past his castle. He even employed pirates to attack the pilgrims on their way across the Red Sea to Mecca. Saladin complained to the Crusader King of Jerusalem, but Reynald would not obey his King. So Saladin at last attacked Reynald's castle of Kerak.

It happened that Reynald's young son and the King's sister had just been married, and Saladin, who did not want to hurt the young couple, ordered his men not to fire at their tower. Saladin did not capture the castle because the King of Jerusalem brought an army to rescue Reynald.

But when Reynald started breaking the truce again and attacking Arab caravans, Saladin prepared a great army. The Crusaders also collected all their knights ready to fight. They should have been well matched, but the Crusaders foolishly entered the battle with their soldiers worn out and thirsty, and Saladin utterly defeated them and took both the King and Reynald prisoner. He beheaded Reynald, but the King and most of the other prisoners he spared. Saladin immediately attacked Jerusalem, which the Crusaders had held for nearly 100 years, and since there were only young boys and old men left to man the walls, Jerusalem soon fell.

When Saladin's army marched in, he gave orders that no one should be hurt, no buildings destroyed, and nothing robbed. His men remembered that when the Crusaders had captured Jerusalem they had killed everyone in the city, but they dared not disobey Saladin. Saladin soon freed all those who could pay a small ransom. The rest

he meant to keep as slaves; but when women came to him begging him to release their husbands, he was sorry for them and did as they asked. In fact, he released more and more prisoners as they passed sadly before him. Although Saladin treated the Crusaders so differently from the way they had treated the Arabs, he was by no means a weak or soft leader. He went on to capture most of the Crusader castles, and he drove the Crusaders back until they held only a few towns on the coast.

The fall of Jerusalem in 1187 started another Crusade from Europe (see Chapter 17). The English King, Richard the Lion Heart, was the sort of soldier whom Saladin respected. They were a match for each other, and each admired the other, for both were brave, chivalrous, and generous. When Richard fell ill of fever, Saladin sent his enemy fruit and snow from the mountains. During the last battle between these two great leaders, when Richard's horse was killed beneath him, Saladin sent a groom through the battle to bring him two magnificent horses. In the end Richard failed to recapture Jerusalem and had to return to England. He brought with him the story of the great Muslim leader, Saladin, by far the most noble figure in the whole history of the Crusades.

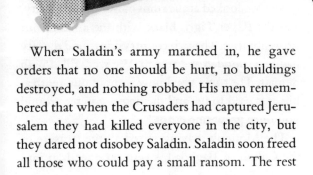

The prisoners' wives begging Saladin to release their husbands

19 THE MONGOL TERROR

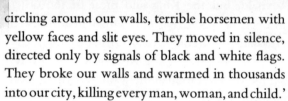

IN THE LATE 13th century there lived an old man in the little town of Baghdad in Iraq, and he had a strange and terrible story to tell. This old man was one of the few survivors of the destruction of Baghdad by the Mongols in 1258. He would sit in the sun on the doorstep of his flat-roofed, sun-dried, mud-brick house, and tell blood-curdling stories to the boys who sat spellbound round him.

The old man told the boys what Baghdad had been like when he was their age. He described the splendid palace where the Caliph had lived, the grand houses belonging to the wealthy merchants or great scholars, the University, a centre of learning for the whole world (see Chapter 14). Also he would describe the rich farmlands round the city, with their fine irrigation systems for bringing water to the fields, and the good crops they grew. 'We thought our city the very centre of civilization,' he said.

But even then dreadful stories were beginning to reach Baghdad. From the east, hordes of fierce Mongol horsemen were galloping across the great open plains from far away, and raiding the countryside, and destroying cities, massacring all the people in them. They were led by the conqueror Genghis Khan, who was marching over all Southern Asia, carrying death and desolation with him. People were so terrified of him that they surrendered without a fight, hoping to save their lives. But the Mongols spared no one. Still they seemed a long way away from Baghdad.

Then news came that the Mongol leader, Hulagu Khan, grandson of the terrible Genghis Khan, had crossed the River Oxus and was heading across Persia, towards Baghdad. 'Our soldiers went out to fight them,' went the old man's story; 'but the Mongols broke our river banks and irrigation dykes, flooded our fields around our soldiers, and charged their horses across the floods to scatter our army.'

'One winter morning,' said the old man, with a strange look of horror in his eyes, 'we saw them circling around our walls, terrible horsemen with yellow faces and slit eyes. They moved in silence, directed only by signals of black and white flags. They broke our walls and swarmed in thousands into our city, killing every man, woman, and child.'

The old man told the boys how he had hidden in the cellar under his house, which had collapsed in the fighting. He crouched there for days, listening in terror to the screams and thuds from above and living on dates which had been stored in the cellar. At last, when all the noise had died down and there was silence, he dug his way out of the cellar. The sight which met his eyes made him wish himself dead. They say that 800,000 people were killed by the Mongols in Baghdad. The Mongols themselves had gone back to their camps outside the city.

'I found the bodies of all my family,' the old man said, 'except my young sister. They must have carried her off as a slave, as they did with many of the young women. I never saw her again. A few people, like myself, had escaped, and together we looked at the ruins of our beautiful city, and the River Tigris black with the ashes of our great libraries. The rich countryside round the city had been flooded and ruined. We were filled with despair. The town you know is about one-tenth as big as it used to be, and the desert you see around you once grew fine crops.'

The Mongols, having seized all the treasure of the Caliph of Baghdad, swept on over Iraq into

Syria, sacked the cities of Aleppo and Damascus, and marched towards Jerusalem. Then two things happened to save the Arab world from the Mongols. The great Khan, the Mongol ruler, died in their homeland 6,000 kilometres away, and much of Hulagu Khan's army turned for home. The rest was defeated by the Muslim commander Baibars, Sultan of Egypt. He drove them out of Syria, and also drove the Crusaders out of the two or three strongholds which they still held (see Chapter 17). But Baghdad never again became the great city it had been.

The Mongols surround Baghdad

20 THE TIGRIS AND EUPHRATES

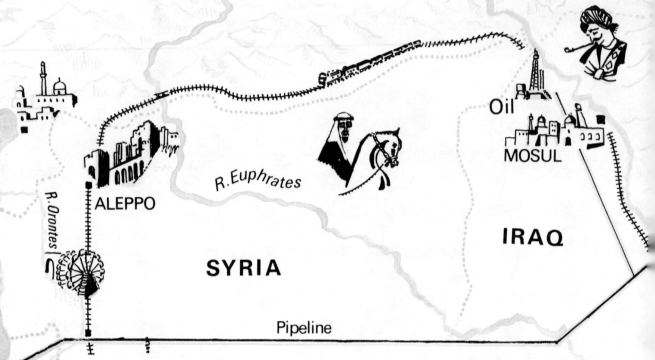

KURDISH MTS

MEDITERRANEAN SEA

R. Orontes

ALEPPO

R. Euphrates

Oil

MOSUL

SYRIA

IRAQ

Pipeline

TRIPOLI

SIDON

BEIRUT

R. Jordan

JORDAN

Jerusalem

IRAQ IS A river land, depending on the great Tigris and Euphrates Rivers which come down from the mountains of Turkey in the north. They flow right across the country, sometimes turning towards each other, sometimes flowing away again, until they join together shortly before they reach the sea. All around them is desert, but the rivers have built up a long plain of rich soil washed down from the mountains, where plants flourish, making the land green.

This river land used to be called Mesopotamia — which means 'land between the rivers'. It is such good land that men came and settled there in very ancient times. It is one of the first places where people, called Sumerians, built cities and learnt to write and organize civilized life over 6,000 years ago (see Book 12). Little is to be seen now of these ancient buildings for, as there was no stone in Mesopotamia, they were built of sun-dried mud bricks, which do not last so well as stone. But the

fame of these cities spread far and wide, and people started to build cities of the same kind elsewhere.

Thousands of years later, the Arabs came to Iraq, and this river valley again became one of the most important places in the world. The Arabs built the city of Baghdad (see Chapter 14) at the point where the rivers come very close together, and they used the rich soil and plenteous supply of water to make magnificent farmlands. One of the difficulties of farming in Mesopotamia was that in the spring, when the snow melted in the mountains, the rivers burst their banks and flooded the countryside. The Arabs did a great deal to control these floods by building high banks, draining the marshes, and making canals and ditches to lead the water away from the rivers to the fields. But the Mongols destroyed in a few months (see Chapter 19) this work which had taken centuries to build up.

The Tigris is the most violent of the two rivers: its spring floods have occasionally washed away large parts of Baghdad. The Bible story of Noah and the flood is probably the story of one of the great Tigris floods, and even as late as 1954 Baghdad was saved from being drowned only by flooding all the surrounding countryside. Today, with the help of British engineers, great dams have been built to hold back the flood water.

Both the Euphrates and the Tigris rise in the Kurdish mountains in Turkey and flow through a fine fertile plain at the foot of the mountains. In winter, the plain is green, and in spring it is a carpet of wild flowers — anemonies, irises, wild hyacinths, lilies, jonquils, and hollyhocks. This is the home of the Kurds, the people from whom Saladin came (see Chapter 18). They bring their flocks of sheep and goats here in the winter and take them up into the mountains in summer. The Kurds are an independent people and a law unto themselves, and their women are not veiled.

The Euphrates flows west through Syria, not very far from the old city of Aleppo (see Chapter 27), and then it turns south-east towards Baghdad. For centuries people travelling from Mesopotamia to the Mediterranean countries and Europe went up the Euphrates to Aleppo, rather than cross the desert, because they could be sure of finding water. So the road from Baghdad to Aleppo was one of the great roads of ancient times.

As they reach the south of Iraq, the rivers spread into a mesh of streams, lakes, and marshes — a world of water and reeds, rich in water birds, and with boats gliding along paths through the reeds, which tower high above them. The people in the marshes use reeds for everything. They build reed houses on an island of reeds and put reed mats over the roofs and on the floors. They even build boats from reeds, and the children build their own little reed rafts and canoes to paddle around in. The village 'street' is a stream, though the water is not very deep. Marsh Arabs cannot keep camels, sheep, and goats as most people do in Iraq. Instead they keep water buffaloes who live on their islands with them, and wallow in the water. The men build up little fields from the mud and grow rice on them, for rice is a crop which likes to be half drowned. In the summer it is hot and steaming, with clouds of mosquitoes.

Beyond the marshes the two rivers join together into one, called the Shatt-al-Arab, which flows to the sea. Along its banks are groves of date palms and the people, and even animals, eat many dates. Ocean-going ships sail right up to the great port of Basra, about 112 kilometres from the sea, and return loaded with grain, dates, wool, cotton, and oil to carry to the rest of the world.

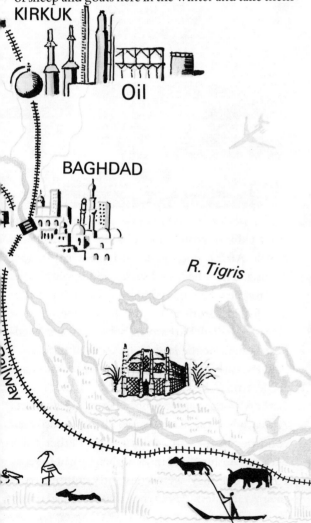

KIRKUK

Oil

BAGHDAD

R. Tigris

MARSH ARABS

SAUDI ARABIA

ABADAN Oil

BASRA

IRAN

Kuwait

Oil

21 PIRATES

ABOUT THE YEAR 1500 a young man from the Eastern Mediterranean came seeking his fortune in North Africa, and he landed in what is now Tunisia. There he found such good opportunities for anyone who enjoyed fighting or piracy that he sent for his brothers to join him. One of these brothers, called Barbarossa, which means 'Redbeard', became the leader of a gang of pirates.

In the early 16th century these pirates had made Algiers their headquarters. Most of them were Berbers — the people who were living in North Africa when the Arab armies drove across their countries in the 7th century. The Berber tribes became Muslims, and most of them learnt to speak Arabic, but they were constantly fighting with their Arab rulers. Also, when the Arabs had finally been driven out of Spain (see Chapter 15), the Spaniards began to make attacks on North Africa. So there was always fighting.

A pirate battle

When they were not fighting the Spaniards or the Arab rulers, the Berber or Barbary pirates attacked ships passing through the Mediterranean. The Spaniards had captured a little rocky island very close to Algiers and built a fort on it. Only after a struggle lasting 14 years did Barbarossa, the pirate leader, manage to drive the Spaniards from this island. Then he built a causeway between the island and Algiers, and this made a very secure harbour. Algiers stands on a curve of high land, so the fort and guns on the mainland could defend the harbour from one side, while the fort and guns on the island protected it from the other. It was a perfect pirate stronghold.

There were also pirates in the Persian Gulf and along the coast of Arabia; they attacked the merchants' ships coming from the wealthy cities on the Tigris and Euphrates (see Chapter 20) and across the Arabian Sea from India and the East. The west coast of the Persian Gulf is ideal for pirates: it is nothing but barren sand dunes hiding creeks and lagoons where pirate boats can lurk. The sea is so shallow that only the light, shallow Arab boats, called dhows, can navigate it. The people of these lands were so poor that many took to piracy to get a livelihood. They were cruel and ruthless, and they could sail their dhows in the light breezes of the Gulf at a great speed.

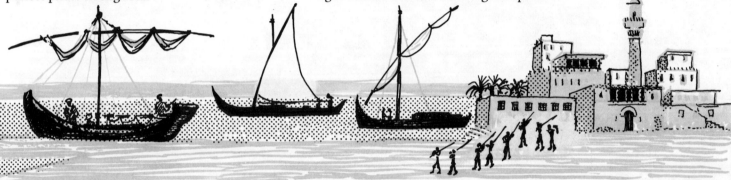

From Algiers the Barbary Pirates built up a pirate kingdom which stretched all along the coast of North Africa and lasted for 300 years. They became so strong that no ships could sail safely along the Mediterranean, and they also made attacks on the coasts of France, Italy, and Spain, plundering the towns and villages. They carried their prisoners back to Algiers, and those not rich enough to pay a high ransom were kept as slaves. At one time there were as many as 20,000 Christian slaves in Algiers alone. At first the pirates rowed their ships, using captured prisoners as oarsmen, chaining them to the oars, and driving them with whips. Later the pirates learnt to use sails, which made them even more the terror of the seas.

At last the French were determined to put an end to the Barbary Pirates. In 1827 they landed an army along the coast, attacked Algiers from land and sea and, after bitter fighting, captured it. Algeria was a French colony until 1962, when it became an independent republic. Now there are no more pirates in the Mediterranean.

The pirates made a headquarters at a fortified village called Ras al Khaima on a sandy shore known as the Pirate Coast. Behind the village lay a hidden creek where the pirate dhows could collect. They would sail from their hideouts at great speed over the shallow water, surround a merchant ship, swarm over her sides, capture her crew, and cut their throats with long, curved knives. Up to 150 years ago they were attacking British ships and, while shouting 'Allah is great', slaughtered their crews. They grew bolder and bolder until at last they even captured a British warship and cut her captain into pieces.

After this, the British sent a strong fleet of ships to Ras al Khaima, captured the fort and village, and destroyed all the pirate dhows. They forced the pirates to sign a treaty giving up piracy, and in exchange undertook to defend their lands from other people. The pirates took up pearl fishing instead, but today, now that oil has been discovered, the old pirate villages have become very rich.

A pirate village

22 THE OTTOMAN TURKS

Constantinople in the 15th century

WE READ IN Chapter 17 how tribes of Turks had for many hundreds of years been moving across the great plains of Asia from near where the Mongols came from, and settling in the countries of Central Asia, which are now part of Russia. (The Turkmen in these countries still speak a Turkish language.) Then the Turks began to spread westwards, over the Arab lands, and in the 10th century they became Muslims, like the Arabs. For a time they were held back by the great Arab ruler Saladin, and then by the Mongols, but in the early 14th century a Turkish leader, Osman, captured most of the land which is now Turkey. Osman became the first Sultan of Turkey, and his people were called the Osmanli, or Ottoman, Turks.

Gradually they conquered all Turkey and threatened Constantinople itself, which had had a Christian Emperor for more than 1,100 years — ever since Constantine the Great had made it his capital. In the year 1453 the Turks conquered Constantinople, and after that, nothing could stop them. They conquered Greece, the Balkan countries, and Hungary, and one by one the Arab countries fell to them. The Turks easily conquered the Arab armies for they had guns, which the Arabs had not. Also the Arabs believed that all that was necessary to win battles was courage, while the Turks had well-organized, well-disciplined armies with leaders who knew how to plan battles.

By the 16th century, under their great Sultan Suleiman the Magnificent, the Ottoman Empire stretched from Persia to the frontiers of Germany, and included all the Arab States, except Morocco, which they never won. With the help of the pirate Barbarossa (see Chapter 21) they captured all North Africa. The Arab world seemed to have come to an end. For 400 years the Arabs were ruled by the Turks, and instead of being the richest and most educated people in the world, they became some of the poorest and most backward.

The Turks changed the name of Constantinople to Istanbul, and from there they ruled their great empire. They did not live in the countries they conquered, as the Arabs had done, but they divided their empire into provinces and sent a governor to each to rule it, and soldiers to keep the peace. The Turks were harsh rulers, but they were very efficient, and at least they followed the same religion as the Arabs.

The Turks had thought of a very successful way of finding enough good rulers and fine soldiers for their huge empire. In the European countries they conquered, they carried off as slaves the strongest, brightest, and best-looking boys and brought them back to Istanbul. They divided them into two groups: the most intelligent, called Pages, and the strongest, called Foreign Boys. The Pages were sent to a Turkish castle where they were given the best possible education, better than most Turkish boys received. Then they worked for a time in the Sultan's palace, learning how the Empire was run. Then, when they were thoroughly well-trained, they were given the important jobs through the empire. Even the position of Grand Vizier (Chief Minister) was given to a slave who had had this training. The Foreign Boys were trained as soldiers and formed a very highly disciplined and trained standing army.

The Arabs in the meantime became poorer and weaker. The Turkish Governors of the Arab countries were more interested in making themselves rich quickly than in making the lands they ruled prosperous, and they taxed the people more and more. Much of the land went back to desert, and the Arab populations grew smaller, and the people more depressed. They could only dream of the glories of the past.

In course of time some of the Governors began to rebel against the Sultan of Istanbul. For instance, in the 19th century, the Governor of Egypt, Mehemet Ali, made himself almost independent of Turkey. Also the Turks were becoming frightened of Russia. At last the Turks were defeated by the Allies in the First World War, and their great empire came to an end. The French and English drove them out of the Arab lands, and for a time ruled these lands themselves (see Chapter 24).

The Bosphorus

51

23 LAWRENCE OF ARABIA

ONE DAY IN 1917 a band of Bedouin Arabs lay hidden below the brow of a hill, with their camels pulled down beside them, and each man with his ear to the ground. At last they heard what they were listening for — the faint sound of an approaching train. Their leader had a box from which wires ran over the hill to the railway line. He waited, finger on the button, until his scout, peering cautiously over the hill, signalled. Then he pressed the button, and immediately there was a deafening roar as the explosion hurled the railway engine from the track. The Bedouin seized their rifles and dashed down, firing wildly, to loot the train.

The Bedouin's leader looked just like the others, thin and brown, with his white robe flapping round his legs and his hair covered with a head cloth. In fact, he was an Englishman called Lawrence, who was helping to lead an Arab revolt against the Turks. The train which he had just blown up was a Turkish train, carrying men and supplies to the Turkish army near Mecca. There was only one railway line from Damascus through Arabia to Mecca, and Lawrence and the Bedouin were blowing it up so often that it could not be used. Distant Arab tribes, who heard of this and did not understand the English name, sent messages asking: 'Please send us a Lawrence so we can blow up trains with it'.

This was during the First World War, when Britain and France were fighting Germany and Turkey. Lawrence, who spoke Arabic, was sent to Arabia to stir up the Arabs to revolt against the Turks. Lawrence needed a leader for the Bedouin tribes in this desert war, and he chose Faisal, the third son of the Sherif of Mecca. Faisal was tall and thin, with a black beard. He had been to school in Turkey, and then had spent many months with the Bedouin in the desert; so he was tough and brave, and the Bedouin loved him.

Faisal and Lawrence meant to capture Damascus; but there were many Turkish soldiers between Damascus and Mecca, and Lawrence thought they should first capture the port of Aqaba (see map p. 9), so that British ships could bring them supplies from the Red Sea. He thought that the only chance was to attack Aqaba from the land by marching across the desert. For days the Arab band rode under the burning sun with little water

Lawrence and his Arabs attacking a Turkish train

and even less food. When they came to a valley where there were plants for their camels and a friendly Bedouin tribe who gave them food, they camped there, but in the morning they found their camp full of snakes which had slid under the blankets beside them for warmth. They rode another long day to where they knew there were wells; but when they arrived nearly dead with thirst, they found that the Turks had blown up the wells. At last they found one well not completely destroyed, which they could clear and obtain water.

Before they reached Aqaba they found that a Turkish force was camped at the top of a high cliff, to the north of the town. They came up behind the camp and charged on the Turks, firing from their saddles, at full gallop. They routed the Turks and triumphantly marched down the cliff towards Aqaba. But they still had to capture the Turkish fort defending the town. Lawrence thought of a very clever way of frightening the Turks and encouraging the Arabs. He knew that there was to be an eclipse of the moon that night. 'Tonight the moon will be dark', he declared, as

though he were a magician able to make the moon obey him. When the eclipse came, the Arabs believed that Lawrence had worked magic, and the Turks were so frightened of the eclipse that they gave in. More and more Arabs joined Lawrence's band, and Aqaba quickly surrendered to them.

The British, realizing how useful the Arabs could be, provided them with aircraft and armoured cars, and Lawrence was able to dash across the desert by car instead of making long, slow camel rides. The British and Arabs together marched north towards Damascus, pursuing the retreating Turks. Lawrence and the Arabs entered Damascus first, and the people greeted them with cheers.

Faisal was made ruler of Damascus, but he found it was not easy to govern. The Arabs of Damascus and the Bedouin of the desert were soon quarrelling, and the British and French meant to rule the lands from which they had driven the Turks. The Arabs found they had exchanged their Turkish masters for British and French ones (see Chapter 24). Faisal left Damascus and later became King of Iraq.

Lawrence went home to Britain disappointed that the Arabs were still not free. He wrote a book called *The Seven Pillars of Wisdom* in which he described all his adventures with the Bedouin people.

24 BRITAIN AND FRANCE RULE THE ARABS

ONE HOT DAY in 1827, the ruler of Algiers, who was also chief of the Barbary Pirates, was so angry with the French Consul, who went to see him to complain about the shipment of a load of wheat, that he struck the Consul with a fly swatter. The Consul stamped angrily out of the ruler's palace, and protested to the French Government. The French immediately sent an army to attack Algiers. In Chapter 21 we read how the French had been growing more and more infuriated with the Barbary Pirates, who attacked their ships and made raids on their lands. They were waiting for an excuse to stamp them out.

Algerian school children doing their lessons in French

When at last the French captured Algiers, they stayed there to govern it so that there should be no more pirates. Gradually they conquered the tribes inland, and across the Sahara Desert as well, until they were ruling a vast country. Algeria was only a short way across the Mediterranean from France, so soon French farmers began to settle in the land near the coast, and to make fine farms.

We also read in Chapter 21 how the British had defeated the pirates of the Persian Gulf, and had signed treaties with the little desert states along the Arabian shore, promising to protect them. So in the 19th century the French were beginning to rule the western end of the Arab world, and the British the eastern end; and soon they were in competition to gain control of the rest of the Arab countries. They felt sure they could run them better than the Turks, who were growing weak and inefficient (see Chapter 22). Also the British wanted to protect their trade routes to India in the east, and the French wanted to protect their own Mediterranean coastland. So each time an Arab country got into any difficulties, the British or French seized the excuse to take over the country. Soon they were ruling most of the countries of the Middle East.

After the First World War, in which Turkey was defeated, it was agreed that Britain and France, who had won the war, should look after the Arab countries until they were able to look after themselves. So the Arabs found themselves under European control. Britain controlled Egypt, Iraq, Jordan, and Palestine; and France ruled Algeria, Morocco, Tunisia, Syria, and Lebanon. The enormous North-African country, Libya, was ruled by the Italians. Only Saudi Arabia and Yemen remained free under their own rulers. Some of the countries had their own kings, but they were not their own masters, as they had hoped to be when the Turks were driven out.

Although the Arabs were disappointed, in fact the English and French did much good in the Arab countries. They built roads, railways, schools, and hospitals. They ran the countries well and peacefully, and brought fair laws and justice. The Arabs began to learn European ways. They were better fed and healthier, fewer children died, and populations began to increase. The ruling families began to send their sons to school in England or France. In Algeria the French treated the country as though it were part of France, and the Arab children did all their lessons at school in French only.

Between the First and Second World Wars, the Arab countries became more prosperous, particularly as it was discovered that under the desert there was oil (see Chapter 25). So when the Second World War was over, all the Arab countries wanted to be free. They did not need the Europeans any more. One by one they were given their freedom. Some, such as Iraq, Syria, Lebanon,

A modern clinic and hospital

But in one country in the Arab world there was no peace. This was Palestine. The Jews wanted to return to their ancient home in Palestine, and the British promised, in return for help during the First World War, to let them do so. So after the War, Jews began to arrive in Palestine, wanting land. But the Arabs thought of Palestine as an Arab country, as it had been for many centuries. There was much bitter fighting, and when the British left Palestine, the country was divided in two. The Arabs have never forgiven Britain for this; they feel that she has given an Arab country away to foreigners (see Chapter 29).

and Jordan, became independent very soon. But the British did not want to leave Egypt altogether because of the Suez Canal (see Chapter 37). The French did not want to leave Algeria for many French people had lived there all their lives. There was a bitter war for 5 years before the French gave Algeria her freedom in 1962. Today all the countries of the Arab world are independent again, though Israel is not Arab and is not accepted by the Arab people. Even the tiny states of the Persian Gulf have become entirely independent of Britain since 1971 — 150 years after Britain took them under her protection.

25 OIL

UNDER THE DESERT sands it has recently been discovered that there is a great treasure: this is oil, which is sometimes called black gold because it is so valuable. Many millions of years ago the deserts were covered by shallow seas full of little fishes, shellfish, and seaweed. When these sea plants and animals died, they dropped to the bottom of the sea, making a thick layer, which in time was covered with more thick layers of sand and rocks. These weighed so heavily upon them that the seaweed and fishes were gradually pressed into thick, black oil.

refine this crude oil so that it could be used to drive ships and all the machines which were being invented in the 19th century. In 1859 the first oil well was dug in Pennsylvania in America. In 1890 a young man called Gulbenkian reported to the Turks that he was sure there was oil to be found in Iraq; but the Arab countries at that time were so wild and dangerous that no one dared to dig wells in the desert. After the First World War, when most of the Arab countries were under the control of Britain and France, the chance to hunt for oil came.

Oil tankers coming to the jetty to take on oil

Here and there people had noticed a strange oily substance oozing out of the ground. In Iraq, for instance, there is a place in the desert where a perpetual fiery furnace was always burning. The fire was fed by gas escaping from a layer of oil under the ground. In some places where oil or tar seeped from the rocks the people living nearby collected it in pots and used it for lining water channels, sealing the gaps between the planks of their boats, or burning when they had no wood for their fires. But no one bothered to find out where the oil was coming from.

In the 19th century it was discovered that if a well was dug in a place where there was oil, deep enough to reach the oil, the oil would come gushish up to the surface. Engineers found out how to

Digging an oil well is an expensive business, for it may have to be dug a mile or more deep. Also there must be roads, and water wells, and houses for the workmen. So it is important to be sure that you find oil. Oil prospecting is like a treasure hunt, when the treasure may be worth millions of pounds. Oil is to be found only in the right kind of rock — rock through which the oil cannot soak. So scientists study the layers of rock under the ground by drilling very deep holes and bringing up samples of the rock to study. Even then no one can tell exactly how deep the oil lies nor how much there is until the well is dug. Some of the wells in Saudi Arabia are 5 kilometres deep.

In many wells the oil gushes out of its own accord; in others, pumps have to be put in the wells to bring the oil up. The well has to have a cap with a series of valves at the top to control the flow of oil. In one of the early wells in Iraq the oil spurted out so high and fast that the engineers could not control it, and it flowed over the countryside. There is a danger that such spurts of oil will catch fire and burn fiercely for a long time.

When the crude oil comes out of the well it has to be refined to clean out of it the water, salt, and mud which are mixed in it. Then it is heated in a high tower called a 'distillation column' to separate off the different kinds of oil — petrol, diesel oil, paraffin, and so on. Each kind is piped out of the tower and carried away separately. Sometimes the oil refineries are near the wells, but much of the oil found in Iraq or Arabia, for example, is pumped through huge pipe-lines for hundreds of kilometres across the desert to the Mediterranean coast or the Persian Gulf. There, the oil is refined and then pumped straight into oil-tanker ships.

The first really big discovery of Arab oil was in Iraq, where Gulbenkian, who bought a few shares in the company, soon became a millionaire. Then an American company found large quantities of oil in Saudi Arabia, and the British found more in Kuwait on the Persian Gulf. After the Second World War oil was found all along the Persian Gulf and in the Sahara Desert in Libya and Algeria. There is probably more oil still under the Arab deserts then anywhere else in the world.

Oil has made all the difference to the people of the Arab world. For instance, there was a very poor village called Abu Dhabi on the Pirate Coast of the Persian Gulf where there were no roads, no schools, few houses, and not much food — just areas of useless desert. In 1962 oil was found there, and now the ruler has so much money he hardly knows what to do with it. Dual carriageway and smart houses are being built and fine new schools. The people can earn a great deal, and in Abu Dhabi even school children are paid, and they earn more for every year they stay at school.

The pipe runs from the refinery across the desert. In front is an oil drill

inspection
nt on the pipe

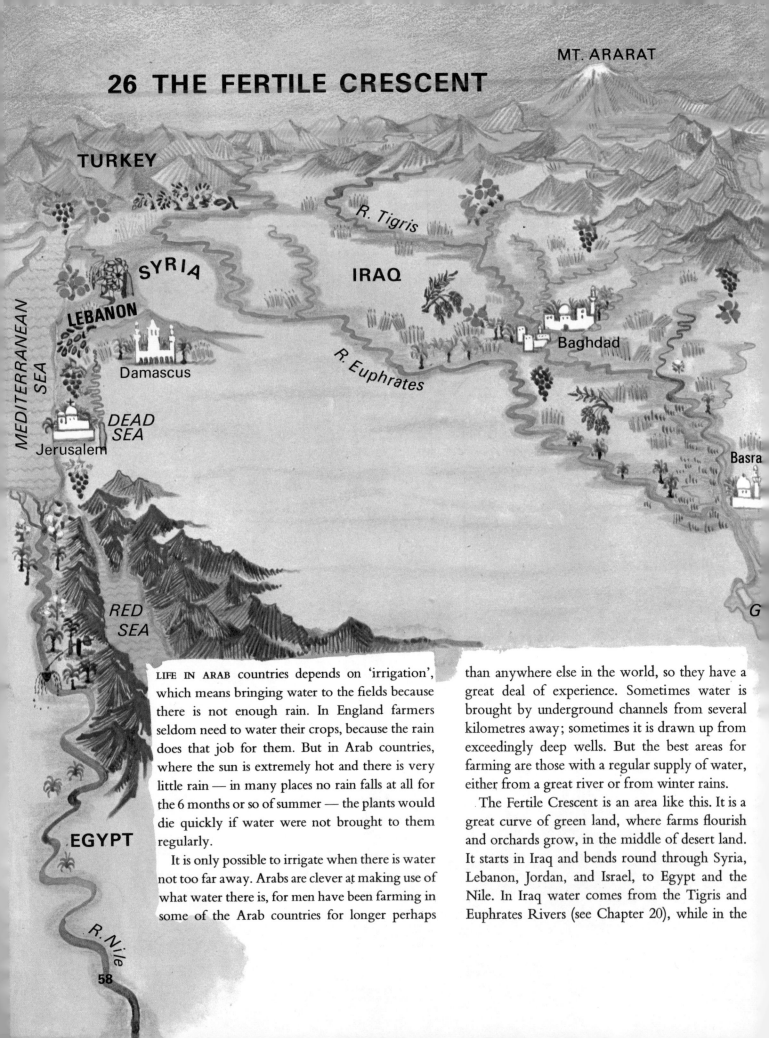

26 THE FERTILE CRESCENT

MT. ARARAT

TURKEY

R. Tigris

SYRIA

IRAQ

LEBANON

MEDITERRANEAN SEA

Damascus

R. Euphrates

Baghdad

DEAD SEA

Jerusalem

Basra

RED SEA

G

EGYPT

R. Nile

LIFE IN ARAB countries depends on 'irrigation', which means bringing water to the fields because there is not enough rain. In England farmers seldom need to water their crops, because the rain does that job for them. But in Arab countries, where the sun is extremely hot and there is very little rain — in many places no rain falls at all for the 6 months or so of summer — the plants would die quickly if water were not brought to them regularly.

It is only possible to irrigate when there is water not too far away. Arabs are clever at making use of what water there is, for men have been farming in some of the Arab countries for longer perhaps than anywhere else in the world, so they have a great deal of experience. Sometimes water is brought by underground channels from several kilometres away; sometimes it is drawn up from exceedingly deep wells. But the best areas for farming are those with a regular supply of water, either from a great river or from winter rains.

The Fertile Crescent is an area like this. It is a great curve of green land, where farms flourish and orchards grow, in the middle of desert land. It starts in Iraq and bends round through Syria, Lebanon, Jordan, and Israel, to Egypt and the Nile. In Iraq water comes from the Tigris and Euphrates Rivers (see Chapter 20), while in the other countries there are hills or mountains where it rains in the winter, and smaller rivers, such as the Jordan, provide water. Along the Mediterranean shores there are green orange groves and vineyards; olive and apple orchards climb up the hill slopes above; and beyond them fine vegetable crops grow in the mountain valleys. Endless grain crops stretch across the plains of Syria, and the best dates in the world grow in Iraq. But these crops would all shrivel up and die unless the farmer knew how to irrigate them.

Fields in the Fertile Crescent are separated from each other by ditches or low banks with water channels running along the tops. The ditches and channels have little gates across them at intervals, which every now and then are opened to allow water to flow along smaller ditches through the fields, or to flood a whole square of field. The water has to be carefully controlled so that no one takes more than his share. When the ditches are filled by water pumped up from a well, then only a certain amount is pumped each day so that the well does not run dry. In summer, when the farmer may be irrigating every day, he often spends much of his time pumping water and opening and shutting the gates of his ditches.

In Lebanon, Jordan, and Israel many crops are grown on the steep slopes of the hills and mountains. Farming here is hard work, for it is difficult to water crops on a steep slope where the water can easily just run away. Also, in winter the rain is often so heavy that the plants and soil may be washed away down the mountain side. So the farmers have learnt by experience to carve their hillsides into a series of giant steps, called terraces. Each terrace is held in place by a stone wall, with a flat surface behind the wall. Water is brought down from step to step in summer, and the walls prevent the soil being washed away in winter.

Between the two mountain ranges of Lebanon runs a deep valley, where the soil is very fertile, and cabbages, melons, carrots, and apricots all grow to a huge size and many other fruits and vegetables grow well. Farmers have grown crops in this valley for a very long time, and today among the fields are the ruins of ancient cities.

The farmer opening the irrigation ditch

Further south, this valley is called the Jordan Valley, along which the River Jordan flows down to the Dead Sea. This sea is really a vast inland lake, nearly 400 metres below sea level, and the lowest place in the world. As the water cannot flow out of the lake, there being nowhere lower for it to go, it stays there and dries out in the hot sun, becoming so salty that nothing can live there; so it is called the Dead Sea. All around it the land is very white because it is full of salt. Beyond is desert, and further south lies Egypt and the Nile. The Valley north of the Dead Sea is full of farms and villages, and ancient places like Jericho — probably the oldest city in the world. When Moses looked down on this valley from the hills above, he knew it was the place which God had promised his people, the Promised Land. But it is probably not as green now as it was when Moses looked down on it

Long ago, farmers in the Fertile Crescent cut down the trees to build houses, and did not plant new trees to take their place. When there are no trees, the land becomes drier, and the soil blows away, and the farms become desert again. This happened in many parts of the Fertile Crescent. Now people have learnt that they must plant trees again, and they are irrigating the land once more, and finding new ways of obtaining water. They build dams on the rivers to hold the winter water for use in the summer, and they put in motor pumps to bring the water up from deep wells. The Fertile Crescent is now producing more and more food to feed the big cities of the Arab lands.

27 ALEPPO

The citadel in Aleppo

ALEPPO IS A big city in the north of Syria (see map p. 9), as big as Damascus, the capital of Syria. Like Damascus, Aleppo is a very old city; it used to be one of the great trading cities of the world. For thousands of years it has stood at the crossroads of trade routes between East and West, North and South. Caravans used to bring goods from China, Persia, Turkey, and Arabia along ancient roads such as that from Baghdad, which ran by the Euphrates River (see Chapter 20). European traders started coming to Aleppo 400 years ago, bringing their goods across the Mediterranean Sea; and the first English merchants came in 1581, when the Levant Trading Company was founded, and Queen Elizabeth I opened one of the first British Consulates in Aleppo to protect her merchants.

In those days Aleppo was a very rich city with fine stone houses, beautiful mosques, schools, and Turkish baths. As well as being beautiful, it was very strongly fortified. In the centre of the city there is a great citadel built on a mound and surrounded by a moat and vast wall. The entrance to the citadel was so strongly defended that only one conqueror has ever captured it by force — the Mongol leader Tamburlaine in 1402.

Today Aleppo is no longer an important trading centre, for trade from the east does not come by caravan across the desert any more. When the Suez Canal was opened (see Chapter 37), trade went by ship, which was quicker and cheaper, and so it no longer passed by Aleppo. So many of the rich merchants' houses in Aleppo are abandoned or pulled down. But it is still a fine city and is a centre of Syria's wool and cotton textile trade.

Aleppo, like most Arab towns, has ancient markets or *souqs*: an enormous rabbit warren of narrow streets twist and turn through the town, with open-fronted shops in alcoves in the walls. In Aleppo the markets are built like tunnels, running downhill from the citadel. It is cool and rather dark inside after the glaring sunshine outside, for the *souqs* are lit only by shafts of sunlight streaming through square openings in the arched roof. The paths are cobbled and not wide enough for carts or cars; but heavily-laden donkeys or mules rattle down them, and sometimes even motor-bikes.

Shops selling the same goods stand side by side. There are groups of shops selling material and ropes for Bedouin tents; others selling cottons, silks, and brocades. There are shoe shops and shops of spices and sweets. There are shops piled high with sheepskins and coats or rugs made of the skins. Each shop is set a little above street level, and the goods are hung round the shop and even across the street. In front is a wooden bench covered with a rug, on which the shopkeeper and his customer sit and bargain over prices. If the shopkeeper asks three Syrian pounds for a skin, the customer will offer one. In the end they will probably agree on two pounds.

Here and there is a magnificent gateway in the wall of the *souq* which leads through to a quiet courtyard, shady with trees. This is a *khan*, an old merchant inn built over 300 years ago, where the caravans coming in from the desert (see Chapter 16) or the foreign merchants from Europe found shelter for the night. There were storerooms for their goods below and bedrooms above. At night a great iron door was shut and all was safe within. The *khans* were once full of life and business; now all is quiet and neglected. A tradesman may carry on his business in a shack in a corner, his family living above, and that is all.

The people of Aleppo are becoming more modern all the time. Many now live in modern apartments in the new suburbs of the city. Most people wear European clothes. The older women still put black veils over their heads and faces when they go out, but of the young ones who go to Government schools, more and more go unveiled.

28 PILGRIMAGE TO MECCA

THE SAND–COVERED BUS rolled on, hour after hour, along the desert road. Inside, the pilgrims dozed in the heat; their luggage was piled above on top of the bus. Old Khalil and his companions, most of them elderly men from Aleppo, had left home 4 days ago and had been travelling steadily southwards, towards Mecca and the heat, ever since.

Khalil's wife had seen him off anxiously. She had heard of the hardships of the *hajj*, the yearly Muslim pilgrimage to Mecca. Her father had told frightening stories of how tiring the pilgrimage was, how hot the sun, and how pilgrims died of exhaustion or fever. But the *hajj* is a religious duty of good Muslims: some Muslims even hope to die during their pilgrimage to Mecca.

When the bus reached Jiddah on the coast of the Red Sea, their pilgrim guide joined them. He would tell them what to do and find them somewhere to sleep. 'About a million pilgrims will be coming to Mecca this year, from all over the world,' he told them. Since the pilgrimage is held only once each year, everyone arrives about the same time — by road, by boat, and the rich ones by plane.

Before they reached Mecca, Khalil and his companions put on their *ihram* or pilgrim dress, which consists of two pieces of white cloth which must have no seams. One piece is wrapped round the waist like a skirt, and the other thrown across one shoulder. Pilgrims wear sandals instead of shoes and nothing on their heads. Before starting, they bathe and have their hair and nails cut.

The pilgrimage really started when they crossed a point, a short way from Mecca, beyond which no one except a Muslim may pass. In Mecca they went straight to the Great Mosque, splendid in its size and rich marble decoration. Khalil saw the courtyard inside the mosque, and suddenly he stood awestruck, for he was looking at the most holy spot in Islam, the Ka'ba — the house of God. He cried out '*Labbayka, ya Rabbi*' ('I am at your command, my Lord'), and he swayed slightly in excitement.

The next day came the ceremony of the Ka'ba. The pilgrims have to run round the Ka'ba three times, and walk slowly round it four times. Each time they must kiss the sacred Black Stone set in a silver mount 1·5 metres up in the granite wall of the Ka'ba. This stone is thought to be a meteorite, and was a centre of pilgrimage before Islam. Khalil joined the mass of pilgrims circling the Ka'ba and managed to push his way through to kiss the Black Stone. But the next time round he could not get near it and had to be content with touching it with his stick. By the seventh time round he was exhausted and dizzy from being pushed about by fresh pilgrims who had just joined the throng. But he was determined to kiss

The courtyard of the Great Mosque and the Ka'ba

pushed his way through the crowd to get a drink of water. In old days there was no water, nor any hospitals for the sick; but now pilgrims are carefully looked after, and the danger of illness is less.

The last day is the Feast of the Sacrifice. The pilgrims go to the village of Mina where they throw stones at three pillars representing devils. Then they each buy a sheep for the sacrifice, for this represents the ram which God sent to Abraham to sacrifice instead of his son. In our Bible (Genesis 22) this son was Isaac, but the Muslims say it was Ishmael. Hundreds of thousands of sheep were sacrificed by the pilgrims, and then they feasted on the meat. But the hot sun and all the slaughter of sheep had taken Khalil's appetite away.

Now the pilgrimage was over, and the pilgrims must make their way home. Khalil put on his own clothes again and then boarded the bus for the long trip home. He was so tired he could scarcely stay awake to see the last of Mecca, but he was completely happy. He sat wrapped in his own joy throughout the long journey, hardly knowing where he was. He had done his religious duty, and earned the title of pilgrim. When he got to Aleppo there would be a triumphant welcome for him and his companions.

the Black Stone once again. Then a man in front of him fell fainting and was carried off, and Khalil was able to approach the Ka'ba.

The pilgrims then visited the shrine of Abraham and the well of Zamzam. In the Muslim version of the Old Testament story (Genesis 21), Hagar came to Mecca with her son, Ishmael, and ran seven times between two hills, searching for water for the dying boy. Then God showed her the well of Zamzam and the boy was saved. The pilgrims act this story again, and they also run seven times between the two hills, along a path now covered with marble arcades. It is nearly a kilometre each way, and Khalil could do little more than walk much of the time.

Then the pilgrims gathered together on the plain of Arafat, 19 kilometres from Mecca, where Adam is supposed to have met Eve. They stood praying and weeping all day in the blazing sun, and Khalil was glad of the umbrella he had brought with him. Even then, by noon he felt faint, and he

63

29 THE HOLY LAND

THE HOLY LAND is the land of the Bible. It is sacred to the Jews because it was the Promised Land to which the prophet Moses had led their ancestors. To Christians it is the land where Jesus was born, grew up, preached, and died. It is also important to the Arabs because in Jerusalem is one of their most sacred shrines, the Dome of the Rock, where Muhammed is believed to have stopped during a miraculous night visit to heaven. The Holy Land is right in the middle of the Arab World.

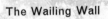

The Wailing Wall

The Dome of the Rock

Today most of the Holy Land belongs once again to the Jews, who call it Israel. Before that, since the 7th century, it had belonged to the Arabs, who called it Palestine. The Arabs believe that the Jews stole it from them, and so they hate Israel. At night, armed bands of Arabs creep across the borders and blow up Jewish farms. Then Israeli soldiers cross into Arab country to take revenge. So raid follows raid, and there is no peace.

The Hebrews (Jews) had settled in Palestine by 1200 B.C. (see Book 12). Soon after Jesus's death, the Romans drove them out, and they were scattered all over the world. Life was never safe for them. They were often persecuted and even killed by the people in whose country they lived. They dreamt of the day when they would have a homeland of their own. During the First World War, Britain offered the Jews a 'home' in Palestine in return for their help in the war. But Britain did not mean to drive out the Arabs; only to let more Jews join the few already living there.

Most of the Palestine Arabs lived on small farms. When the Jews began to arrive, the Arabs feared there would not be enough land for everyone. So the British, who were responsible for ruling Palestine after the First World War, allowed only a certain number of Jews to come to Palestine each year. But when Hitler began to persecute the Jews in Germany, they fled, if they could, to Palestine, and more and more Jews arrived in this small country. The Nazis killed six million Jews in Europe. After the Second World War, the Jews in Palestine were determined to save any of their relatives left alive in Europe and to bring them to Palestine. They were prepared to fight to get enough land for them; the Arabs fought too to save their homes; and both sides fought the British. The British handed over this difficult problem to the United Nations, and British troops left Palestine in 1948. The United Nations said that the country should be divided in two — one part for Arabs, the other for Jews — but this satisfied neither side.

The Jews immediately announced that part of the country, which they called Israel, was theirs. They knew they would have to fight for it, but they had prepared for war. The Arab countries nearby sent armies to try to win back Palestine, but they did not succeed. Neither side could push the other out of Jerusalem. Finally the United Nations stopped the fighting, and drew a frontier line between the two armies. Since both Jews and Arabs were still in Jerusalem, they ran the line right through the middle of the city.

Most of the Arabs who had been living in Israel fled during the war, becoming homeless refugees, though about 200,000 stayed in Israel. Jordan allowed the refugees to live in huts in vast refugee camps. But Jordan is a poor country, and she could not find work for them all. The United Nations gave them food, and there they stayed, hoping some day to return home. No Arab country would give them a home because they would not accept that they could not go back to Palestine. But their homes in Palestine no longer existed.

The Jews have made Israel into a quite different country from the Palestine of old, and Jews in America and Europe gave them money. Israel is now more like a European than an Arab country, for many highly-educated Jews from Europe have come there. There are clean, modern towns with new buildings and factories with complicated machinery. The people are dressed like European people, and women do the same jobs as men. The Israelis had to grow food for themselves in this new land, so the Israeli Government set up farming villages, called *kibbutzim*, where everyone works together on a general plan, instead of each man working for himself. In this way they have turned much desert into good productive farms. Israel is a small country, but it has become very strong, and its people are tough and hardworking.

The Arabs still hope to win Palestine back, and still they will not agree that Israel exists. The name Israel is crossed out in Arab books, and no Arab maps show Israel on them. In 1967 war broke out again between Israel and the Arabs; the Israelis defeated the Arabs in a few days, and captured more land, including the whole of Jerusalem. This has only made many Arabs even more determined than ever to drive the Jews out of the Arab World in the end.

Arab refugees made homeless by the fighting

The square in front of the Church of the Holy Nativity

MUSA IS THE son of a carpenter in Bethlehem. He is 9 years old and lives above his father's shop with his parents, his sister Ibtisām (which means 'smiling') and his little brother Alex. Their home is in an old street very near the place where Jesus was born nearly 2,000 years ago. Musa knows all about that, for he is a Christian; his name means Moses in English.

Musa's father, Issa, works in a small, dark shop which has no windows. The only day-light comes through the wide doors, standing open on to the street, though now they have electric light too. Issa carves statues of the Holy Family in olive wood, and sells them to the foreign tourists who come to visit Bethlehem. It used to take a long time to make one statue, for olive wood is very hard, but now Issa has a machine. This cuts out six rough statues at a time, and then Issa and the others who work with him polish them and put in the details by hand. Issa himself works on the faces, which are the most difficult and important part.

The boys are playing jackstones

While little Alex plays barefoot in the streets all day, Ibtisām goes to a private high school, and Musa goes to a primary school. His school is much like an English school, except that the classes are very big and there are not so many games. Musa had just started to learn English, and he likes to talk it with any tourist who will speak with him, for English is an important language for anyone who wants to get a good job in Bethlehem. Many of the boys are Moslems and go to the mosque on Fridays, and others go to the Christian church on Sundays. So there is no school on either Fridays or Sundays because about half the people in Bethlehem are Christians and half Moslems.

Musa's favourite game out of school is jackstones, which you play with little square stones from the countryside. These were once part of Roman mosaic floors made centuries ago, and some of them are coloured.

Bethlehem is still a small town, although it has grown a great deal recently. It is a white town, built on a line of white hills. Round about it there are green olive groves and fields where sheep graze, but further away the green fades into a yellowish-white, barren landscape, and bare hills roll away into the distance. In the centre of the town, high on a hill, stands a great church which was built about 1,600 years ago to mark the place where Christ was said to have been born.

The only doorway into the church is so low that even Musa has to bend down to go through it. Once the church had a high door, but when the Turks ruled Bethlehem, Turkish horsemen used to ride right into the church, so the door was made so small that they could not do this. Inside, the church is very high, with tall, painted Roman columns. Just beside the altar a narrow flight of dark steps leads down into a little cave which was the stable where it is thought Jesus was born. There is too little wood near by to build sheds, and so animals are stabled in caves. The cave looks very different from how it looked when Mary and Joseph came there. Then it was a simple cave, like others around Bethlehem, with a sandy floor and smoke-blackened ceiling. Now it is lined with white marble and tapestries, with a marble

The cave where Jesus is said to have been born

manger, and a silver star near it set in the marble floor, and is lit by many elaborate lamps.

There is a large mosque across the square from this church, and along the hills at night the lights of the people of a third great religion can be seen: Judaism of the Jews. The land to the west of Bethlehem belongs to the Jews and is called Israel (see Chapter 29). Musa is afraid of the Israelis. Some of his friends, who used to live in what is now Israel, live in a refugee camp on the outskirts of Bethlehem because their old homes now belong to the Israelis. Life in Bethlehem is insecure nowadays because there is bitter enmity between the Arabs and Jews.

In old days the people of Bethlehem all wore long Arab robes, and some men used to wear the red Turkish fez on their heads. Today many people dress just like people in England, though many still wear old-fashioned clothes. Musa notices that usually it is the richer people who wear western clothes and live in modern houses and own cars. He and his friends work hard at school because they want to have good jobs when they are older, and become part of the new world in Bethlehem.

31 A VISIT TO JERUSALEM

A street in Old Jerusalem

'TODAY WE WILL go to Jerusalem,' said Musa's father one July day when they were on holiday. They set off by bus from Bethlehem. The road runs across the white hills of Palestine to Jerusalem, which is only 8 kilometres away. They saw the old walls of Jerusalem across a valley on their left. On their right was the Mount of Olives, from which Jesus ascended to heaven, and at its foot the Garden of Gethsemane where he often went to pray with his disciples. The bus drove alongside the huge wall, behind which lies the old city. On the other side of the road is a modern part of the city.

Musa and his family got off the bus and turned left down a flight of steps leading to a great gateway in the old wall. This is the Damascus Gate, one of the few gates in the old city walls which are kept open; most of the gates were barred long ago, or when Jerusalem was divided into two cities, between the Arabs and Jews. Up and down the steps to the gateway merchants were selling their wares, and women were selling eggs and vegetables from baskets covered with goat hide, which they balanced on their heads.

Through the gate they seemed to enter a different, more ancient world. The narrow streets were packed with people. No cars, not even carts, can drive in these streets, which are sometimes so narrow that one can stretch one's arms right across them. Soon the street becomes roofed over, and they passed from brilliant sunshine into shade, cut by rays of sunlight from openings in the arches above. Flies and dust swirled in the beams of light. Tiny shops open straight onto the narrow street, like caves opening off a tunnel. They reminded Musa of Aleppo, where he had once been (see Chapter 27). A cobbler mending sandals was squeezed in between his sewing machine in front of him and shelves of tools behind. Next door was a butcher's shop with a sheep's and a camel's head hanging outside to show what meat was for sale. The street was hot and smelly and full of flies. A

porter jostled past them carrying about fifteen crates on his back, held in place by a strap over his forehead. On the floor against the wall a row of Bedouin women sat cross-legged, with their baskets of eggs, vine leaves, and yoghurt; and some of them held babies asleep in their laps.

Musa and his family turned right up the Via Dolorosa, a steep street along which Jesus is supposed to have carried his cross to Calvary. The street goes in steps up to the great Church of the Holy Sepulchure, which has been built on the spot where it is thought that Jesus was buried, and is the most important church for Christians. Much of what we can now see was built by the Crusaders (see Chapter 17), and on a wall there are hundreds of little crosses which they carved. The church is round, and in the centre is the huge tomb of Christ, inside which is a marble slab marking Christ's grave. It all looks new, and not at all as it must have looked when Christ was buried there. Each part of the church belongs to a different Christian sect, each with its own altar. These are very elaborate with a great many statues and pictures and candles. One altar, up some steps, is thought to mark the place where Christ was crucified — the hill of Calvary, though no one knows for certain where this was. The whole church smells of incense.

Then Musa's father took them to see the holy places of the Jews and of the Muslims, for Jerusalem is a sacred place for all three religions. Both Jews and Muslims hold sacred the same spot, a hilltop where King David built an altar on a big rock, about 3000 years ago, and where Muhammad is said to have been led in a dream and taken up to heaven. When the Arabs built a mosque on the holy rock, and then a high wall to keep the Jews away, the Jews came to this wall to lament and pray. It came to be called the Wailing Wall, and it is a most important Jewish holy place.

The children climbed the steps to a wide courtyard round a mosque called the Dome of the Rock. 'This is one of the most beautiful buildings in the world,' their father said, 'a splendid example of Arab architecture.' The mosque is covered outside with white marble and blue and white tiles, and exactly above the sacred rock is a huge golden dome. People must take off their shoes when they enter a Muslim mosque, and women must cover their heads. Inside the mosque is a round hall with carpets on the floor, but no seats, and mosaics and gold patterns decorate the walls. In the middle, behind a wooden railing, is the great rock. The Dome of the Rock is one of the holy places all Muslims wish to visit at least once during the course of their lives.

A view of Jerusalem from the Bethany road

BEIRUT IS THE capital of the Lebanon (see map p. 9), a little mountainous country lying on the eastern shores of the Mediterranean between the sea and Syria. Between the steep, dark, pine woods and the sea there are some flat strips of land, where bananas, oranges, lemons, grapefruit, and olives grow very well. The towns of Lebanon are built along the coast, and some, such as the Phoenician towns of Tyre and Sidon (see Book 12), were very ancient.

Beirut is a big white city built on a rocky promontory which juts out into the sea. On three sides the sea laps against the rocks at the foot of the buildings, and on the fourth the land rises to mountains. One third of the people in Lebanon live in Beirut, which is often called 'the gateway of the Middle East' because it is important to the whole of the Middle East, and has one of the best harbours for ships on the eastern Mediterranean coast. It has a busy international airport where planes land and take off throughout the day and night. People and goods come through Beirut on their way to and from the neighbouring countries.

According to a legend, St George killed the dragon in Beirut in the 3rd century, when Christians were being persecuted. When, some 800 years ago, a band of Crusaders landed at Beirut, they said that they saw the figure of St George floating over the bay, which to this day is still called St George's Bay. They took the story of St George home with them, and he became the patron saint of England.

Beirut was originally a small Phoenician town. The Romans made it important, and built a famous law school there. Many Romans came to live in Beirut. But almost all the old town was destroyed by a terrible earthquake in A.D. 551. The city of today is modern: great concrete blocks of flats and business houses tower up towards the sky, and wherever there is room, more are being built. Older houses and their gardens are being destroyed to make space for flats. The streets are no wider than is necessary to take the crowded, noisy traffic. Many of the cars have red number plates; these are taxis, and people use them all the time for they are very cheap. Everyone in Beirut drives very fast, and the smashed-up bodies of cars often litter pieces of waste ground between the buildings.

Beirut is a city of very smart shops, selling goods from all over the world, which it can import because it is full of very rich merchants and bankers; these people grow richer all the time because they do not have to pay high taxes, as people in Europe do. But some of the people in this rich town are very poor indeed. These people live in shacks made of petrol cans and bits of corrugated iron and anything else they can find, in among the pine woods at the edge of the town. They hang their washing up to dry on the barbed-wire fences, and their children play in the dirt round their huts, which in winter are sometimes flooded. Some of the very poor people were refugees from Palestine (see Chapter 29). They cannot afford a proper house or flat in Beirut where everything, especially houses, is expensive. They have no money to buy goods brought from other lands, and they live on the simplest food, mostly bread, olives, yoghurt, and cheese.

St. George fighting the dragon from a Russian icon

There are some parts of Beirut which still look like an Arab town, and here there are older houses, markets in the street, plenty of noise, colour, and untidiness, and people still wearing long Arab gowns. On the whole the people who live in the old parts are Muslims, whereas the people in the newer districts are usually Christians. The older districts are becoming smaller all the time as new buildings go up round about them, and sometimes even in the middle of them.

Life in Beirut is quite different from life in other Arab towns, such as Aleppo and Damascus. Here, people do not live gently, sitting in the sun for much of the day. They hurry about and work long hours, as people do in European towns. Men and women wear European clothes, and women are free to go about by themselves as they please. Most people speak French or English as well as Arabic, and there are schools and universities in French and English for their children. The Lebanese are more interested in the rest of the world than any other Arab people, and many Lebanese have gone abroad to seek their fortune. In fact, there are now as many Lebanese living in other countries as there are in Lebanon itself; but these people keep in touch with their relatives, and many come back to Beirut from time to time. Also many foreigners have come to live in Beirut. For example Armenians own many of the small shops, and there are many American and European businessmen. Though Beirut is still an Arab city, it has followed the ways of the rest of the world.

33 THE NILE VALLEY

THE NILE IS probably the longest river in the world; it is certainly the most famous. It rises in East Africa and flows over 6,400 kilometres northwards to the Mediterranean Sea. Its little streams start in hot, wet countries, but the river itself flows through desert. From the cloudless blue sky above, it looks like a great, green snake, wriggling across the yellow sand. For thousands of years it has given life to the parched lands of the northern Sudan and Egypt.

The White Nile, the longest branch of the river, enters the Sudan through hot, damp swamps, called the Sudd, where there are more crocodiles and hippopotamuses than people. It is difficult to sail boats down the river here, because it is always becoming blocked with floating masses of grass and reeds and tangled roots. Sometimes a special ship has to be sent to cut a passage through. The people of the swamps paddle their way through the reeds in dug-out canoes. Arabs used to capture these people and sell them as slaves. They are tall and black, and wear either no clothes or perhaps a loin cloth. They live very simply, much as they have always done. They fish with nets, hunt animals with spears, and keep cattle. After the swamp comes the savanna, open plains where the grass often grows higher than a man, and where elephants, lions, giraffes, antelopes, and other animals roam.

In the middle of the Sudan stands Khartoum, the big, modern capital city of the Sudan. Here the river is joined by the Blue Nile, which has come down from the highlands of Ethiopia. The word 'Sudan' means 'land of the blacks', but the people of Khartoum are partly Arab, speak Arabic, wear European or Arabic clothes, and live much like the Egyptians; they are quite different from the Negro people to the south.

In the high plains of Ethiopia, from where the Blue Nile comes, there is plenty of rain in summer, so in summer and autumn the river carries a great deal of rain water, and with it a very fine mud called silt. The flood water carries the silt over the fields all along the Nile valley; and as the water drains away, the silt is left on the fields, building up very fertile soil, on which the people of the Nile valley have grown crops for thousands of years. The Nile winds across the desert through an area where it hardly ever rains. Northern Sudan and southern Egypt are among the driest places in the world; in some districts it may not rain for 10 years at a time. A young child there might never have seen rain. The river sometimes falls over cataracts and rapids where boats cannot pass, but it gradually becomes more sluggish and mud-coloured as it reaches the frontiers of Egypt. Along

An imaginary picture showing the buildings and animals and people you might have seen along the Nile Valley from Cairo to the swamps

72

the 1,200 kilometres through Egypt to the sea, wide, flat boats called *feluccas* carry goods up and down the country. They have one large, triangular, white sail, and are often so heavily loaded that they seem about to sink.

The river flows through a narrow valley to Aswan; then the green strip of cultivated fields and groves of date palms on either side of it widens, sometimes up to 18 kilometres wide. Beyond, on either side, are low, rolling, sand dunes stretching away in both directions, with only an occasional oasis (see Chapter 5) to interrupt the endless miles of yellow sand. There are hardly any wild animals — only the farmers' donkeys, camels, buffaloes, and cows.

After the Nile has passed the city of Cairo, the capital of Egypt, it divides into two branches, and reaches the sea through a broad delta. This is a great triangle of green land, where rich crops grow between the arms of the river. It has been built up through the centuries by silt carried down from the mountains by the river.

The land of the Nile valley is some of the most fertile land in the world, and the cotton and wheat fields produce very fine crops. In olden days, every summer, after the Nile floods had covered all the fields with a shallow coating of chocolate-coloured mud, and the water had drained away, the peasants sowed their seeds on the mud. Then they found that, by digging irrigation ditches and bringing water from the river to the fields, they could make a second crop grow before the next flood came. But there was always the fear that the river might not bring enough water or that it might bring too much. Today, however, now that the High Dam at Aswan is built (see Chapter 38), the Nile no longer floods, and there is always the right amount of water.

The Nile is famous because along its banks were some of the first places where men learnt to farm and to build cities. When people were still living as savages in most parts of the world, the ancient Egyptians were making laws, writing books, painting, and also creating temples and statues which are still standing today. This wonderful civilization is described in Book 12 in this series.

Nadia's home
in Egypt

NADIA IS A small, thin girl of 9, with long, black hair and a pale face. Like her brothers and sisters, she wears a *galabia*, a striped cotton gown down to her ankles, and silver earrings. She lives with her father and mother and five brothers and sisters in a house built of brown mud bricks, with a flat roof, in an Egyptian village in the Nile valley. Her house has just plain walls with a few small holes for windows, and one entrance leading into a small yard. Round the yard are small, dark rooms for Nadia's family, her uncle's family, and their animals. On the flat roof are piles of sticks, animal dung which is used for fuel, and storage bins made of sun-baked mud. Inside the house there is very little furniture, and what there is is mostly made of baked mud. Nadia's mother, for instance, has a cupboard, a storage bin, and a low pedestal on which she can stand a tray. There are mats on the floor on which the family sit and sleep.

Nadia spends most of her day indoors looking after her 2-year-old brother, whom she carries round on her shoulder, or in her arms when he is sleeping. She is worried about her little brother because last year another baby brother became ill and died, and this one looks pale and listless, and in the summer the flies settle in black swarms on his eyes. The clinic tells her to keep him clean and protect his face from the flies. But her mother is afraid that if he looks too clean and pretty he may attract the Evil Eye. She tries to make him better by having someone say charms over him, and she tells Nadia to make blue hand prints on the walls to keep away the Evil Eye. But more and more people nowadays are paying attention to what they are told at the clinic, and fewer children die or go blind.

Nadia has two older brothers who are out most of the day. Mahmoud, who is 13, works with his father in the fields. He does most of the farm work now, for their father has an illness called bilharzia, which makes him tired. Most Nile-valley peasants catch this disease from the water in the canals, in which they are always working, and it makes them always feel tired. Muhammad, Nadia's second brother, goes to school, and after school he helps in the fields. Nadia ought to go to school too, but she quite often does not go; her father says there is no point in girls learning to read, so he keeps her at home to help her mother. He kept his eldest son from school much of the time to help in the fields; but he is proud that his second son can read and write well.

The village is built on a slight mound so that, in old days when the River Nile used to flood, it was above the water (see Chapter 33). Date palms grow round the village and give some shade. Most of the houses are like Nadia's, and there are narrow paths of beaten mud between them, which are often littered with rubbish. There is a rich farmer in the village who has a finer house, painted white outside. He has a strip painted over his door with scenes describing his pilgrimage to Mecca (see Chapter 28). There is also a new white building for the school, and another for the clinic and community centre, where the villagers can see a doctor or nurse and where they gather for classes — home crafts for the women and farming for men.

The day's work starts at dawn when the call to prayer comes from the minaret of the village mosque. The men go off to the fields with their animals, taking their breakfast with them. They still use tools which peasants in Egypt have used for thousands of years: a wooden plough pulled by a buffalo and cow, a hoe, and a short sickle for cutting the crop. They grow maize and vegetables, clover for the animals, and a little cotton to sell. The most important job is pumping water for irrigating the fields. This is done with a water wheel on which buckets are fixed, and which is turned by one of the animals; or sometimes they use a screw pump, which has to be worked by hand.

At noon they stop work and sit in the shade eating the lunch Nadia brings them, and often listening to a transistor. In the evening they come back to the house for a meal and then go out into the village street to talk with the other men of the village. No women ever go to these gatherings. The meal is usually a stew of beans, onions, and rice, with home-made coarse bread, cheese, and water, which Nadia has carried back from the village pump in a big stone jar balanced on her head. On feast days, at harvest, for example, they have some meat, chicken, or pigeon; but when food is short, they may have to go hungry.

A farmer ploughing with a camel and a water buffalo

35 PRESIDENT NASSER OF EGYPT

IN THE EARLY morning on 23rd July, 1952, a band of young officers of the Egyptian army surrounded the palace of King Farouk, forced their way in, and made the king give up his throne and leave Egypt altogether. It was only later that people found out who was the real leader of the officers. It was a young man of 34 called Gamal Abdul Nasser, the son of a post-office clerk.

King Farouk, whose family had ruled Egypt since Mehemet Ali (see Chapter 22), was not an Egyptian. In fact, Egypt had not had a truly Egyptian ruler since the days of the Pharoahs. The foreigners who had ruled Egypt had often grown very rich, while the people of Egypt remained extremely poor. King Farouk was both rich and fat, and his rule did not help the peasants.

These young army officers had been planning for a long time to lead a revolution and to free their country from selfish kings and foreign soldiers. Britain had had soldiers stationed in Egypt for about 70 years, mainly to protect the Suez Canal (see Chapter 37), and the officers were particularly determined to make the British leave Egypt.

Gamal Abdul Nasser had been sent to school, and afterwards to a military college to train as an officer in the Egyptian army. He spent his time thinking of one thing — how he could free his country from foreigners, and he saw himself as a great leader. He began secretly to organize a group of friends who thought as he did. At last his group was large enough and well enough organized to be ready to attack, and so on that July morning they brought about a revolution in their country without any fighting at all.

In 1967 Nasser again provoked Israel by threatening the Gulf of Aqaba with big guns, proposing to shoot any Israeli ships which used the Gulf. Again the Israeli army invaded Egypt. They defeated the Egyptians in 5 days, and marched over Sinai as far as the Suez Canal; and this time they refused to withdraw. The result is that now no one can use the Suez Canal, which is blocked and silting up, and Egypt has lost the income she used to get from the Canal.

Having banished the king, Nasser quickly made himself ruler of his country, and within 4 years he was President of the Egyptian Republic. He set to work to take over businesses and factories from their owners and to distribute the land of rich people, especially foreigners, among the peasants. He needed money for improving the lives of the Egyptian people, for giving them better food and doctors and schools, and especially for his great scheme to build a new dam on the Nile (see Chapter 38). He borrowed money from other countries, and also he made up his mind that Egypt — not Britain and France — should own the Suez Canal. The British, French, and Israelis invaded Egypt in 1956 to stop his doing this, but, as we shall read in the next chapter, Nasser succeeded in getting control of the canal.

But Nasser was not content with just being ruler of Egypt; he wanted to unite all the Arabs and be a leader for the whole Arab world. For a time Syria joined Egypt to form the United Arab Republic, but this lasted only 3 years. The other Arab countries did not want to be led by Nasser. Then, like all Arabs, he wanted to drive out the Israelis. He would not let Israeli ships use the Suez Canal, and he also tried to prevent their using the Gulf of Aqaba to reach their own port of Eilat. So the Israelis attacked Egypt. The United Nations made them go home, but allowed them to use the Gulf of Aqaba (see map p. 9).

Although Nasser was defeated by the Israelis, he was still followed by his own people who did not allow him to resign, and he did a great deal to make life better for them. He was respected by other countries, and he made Egypt the leading country in the Arab world. When he died, other Arabs as well as Egyptians looked upon him as the one person who could solve their problems.

36 CAIRO AND ALEXANDRIA

The city of Cairo

CAIRO IS THE capital of Egypt, and the biggest and most important city in the Arab world, with a population of nearly 5 million people. It stands on the banks of the Nile, filling the valley from east to west. To the south the Nile valley winds away through the desert, and to the north it widens out into the delta, with its patchwork of green fields.

Some of the earliest civilizations of the world existed in Egypt, and the ancient Egyptians (see Book 12) built two great cities near where Cairo now stands. The Romans built a fortress there, and in 641 an Arab general began to build a town near the fortress. About 300 years later a new walled town was built, and many of the stones for the walls were taken from the Pyramids, which tower above the edge of the town. These stones, with their ancient Egyptian carvings, can still be

seen in the walls of old Cairo. This city was called Al Qahira, from which comes the modern name Cairo. In the 12th century Saladin (see Chapter 18) greatly enlarged the city, and built a fine fortress on a rock overlooking the east side of Cairo. After the Turks conquered Egypt, until Mehemet Ali ruled the country (see Chapter 22), Cairo grew little, but in the last 100 years a great modern city has grown up, and today the towers and minarets of many beautiful old mosques rise up among Cairo's modern buildings and beautiful parks.

The whole city is coated with the brown dust of Nile mud, for as it rains only three or four times a year, the buildings are rarely washed clean. But the people who fill Cairo's busy streets provide splashes of bright colour against the brown background. Most boys wear blue or green and white striped pyjamas, and girls wear long, flowered cotton dresses, perhaps with different coloured trousers beneath them. The older women often wear long black dresses, with black cloths over their hair, but they are not usually veiled.

The streets of Cairo are always crowded. Jostling, noisy masses of people thread their way among the stalls set up on the pavement, and men

sit outside the shops and houses on chairs, or sometimes simply on the ground, and at midday many of them find a quiet place on the pavement and lie down and go to sleep. Cars hoot continuously at pedestrians walking unconcernedly among the busy traffic, or at errand boys on bicycles balancing large trays of bread or other goods on their heads. Carts with huge wheels, which have come in from the countryside, rumble through the crowded city centre, and buses and trams add to the general confusion. In the back streets chickens may be pecking about and children playing, or a group of women all in black may be sitting on mats outside a house wailing because someone has died in the house.

This bustling city with its modern business houses is also a centre of learning. The Al Azhar university, founded in the middle ages and built around a mosque, is the principal university for studying the religion of Islam in the Arab World. In the great hall, teachers used to sit by the pillars, surrounded by bare-footed students, either learning the Koran by heart or studying its teaching.

In the modern university of Cairo students from many countries study all kinds of subjects.

Alexandria, Egypt's great port, stands on the Mediterranean coast north of Cairo. It is a much more European city than Cairo and, until recently, has had more foreigners than Egyptians living in it. Its straight streets, which run from north to south so that the wind from the sea can sweep them clean, are very different from the streets of Cairo.

Alexandria was built by the Greek conqueror, Alexander the Great, in 331 B.C. It was built partly on the island of Pharos, which was linked to the mainland by a harbour wall; and a splendid lighthouse was built at the entrance to the harbour. The Pharos lighthouse, the first of its kind, was called by the Greeks one of the seven wonders of the world, and it has been a pattern for lighthouses ever since. The French word for 'lighthouse' is *phare*. It was also the model for the minarets of Arab mosques, and the Arabic word for 'lighthouse' is *manarat*. One of the greatest libraries of the ancient world was at Alexandria, but this was destroyed long before the Arabs came to Alexandria.

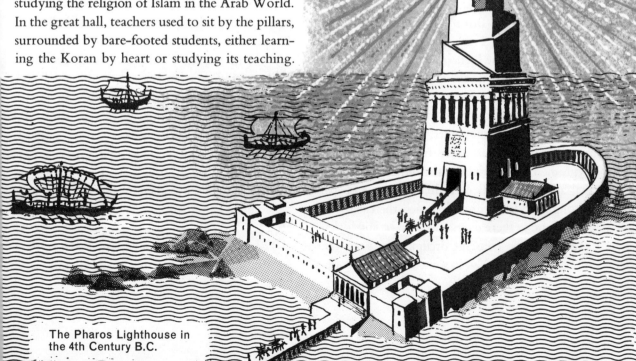

The Pharos Lighthouse in the 4th Century B.C.

37 THE SUEZ CANAL

IF YOU LOOK at a map of the world, you will see that Africa is joined to Asia, and the Mediterranean separated from the Red Sea and the Arabian Sea, by a narrow neck of land. Before 1869 anyone wanting to travel, for example, to India, or to bring a cargo of spices from the far East to Britain, either had to go the whole way round South Africa or had to leave their ship at Port Said in the Mediterranean, cross over this strip of land, and take another ship the other side.

For centuries people had the idea of cutting a canal through this neck, so that ships could sail from the Mediterranean right through to the East. In ancient times the Egyptians did dig a canal from the Red Sea to the river Nile, but this had filled with sand long ago. In later times people were afraid that if a canal were dug from the Red Sea to the Mediterranean, all the water in the Red Sea would pour into the Mediterranean and flood the lands round it, because they thought that the Red Sea was about 12 metres higher. At last, in 1859 a young French Engineer called Ferdinand de Lesseps produced a plan for digging a canal.

De Lesseps was a friend of the ruler of Egypt, who was very keen that the canal should be built, even though people said it was impossible. He promised to put up money and to find workmen. The French also were interested and put up a lot of money. But the British Government did not like the idea at all. They were afraid that if the canal were built, the French would be able to sail too easily across the world, and the British would lose command of the seas.

In 1859 de Lesseps started work on his canal. It took him 10 years altogether, and he had many difficulties to overcome. His friend, the ruler of Egypt, died, and the next ruler did not want the canal and made endless troubles for de Lesseps. Although the land through which the canal ran was flat, and so there did not have to be any locks, there had to be constant dredging to keep the canal clear of sand. Also in some places the work-men had to blast through great masses of granite rock. The canal is 166 kilometres long, and de Lesseps made two lakes out of marshy hollows, where ships could pass each other. At last, in 1869, the Suez Canal was opened, and the first ship, a French one, sailed through from the Mediterranean to the Port of Suez and the Red Sea.

When the Canal was finished, the British realized how useful it could be to them too. For instance, the canal shortened the journey from Britain to India by 6,400 kilometres, and to Australia by 1,900 km. When de Lesseps went to London, a great fuss was made of him. However, the ruler of Egypt was so extravagant that he had to sell his shares in the Canal to pay his debts, and the British Government bought them. Now the Canal belonged mainly to Britain and France, and in 1882, when Britain gained control of the whole of Egypt, she stationed soldiers at both ends of the Canal to protect it and to see that it was managed efficiently. In 1948, of the 8,868 ships which passed through the Canal, more than half were British. In 1955, 14,660 ships passed through, a great many of them tankers carrying oil from the Persian Gulf.

When Egypt became independent, and Nasser became ruler (see Chapter 35), he was determined to get rid of foreign soldiers from the Canal. It had been agreed that the Canal should become Egyptian by 1968, but Nasser would not wait; and in 1956 he suddenly announced that the Canal belonged to Egypt, and that it would now be run by Egyptians. He also refused to let the Israelis use it. The British and French were very angry, for they did not trust the Egyptians to run it properly or to have enough experienced pilots to be able to guide ships safely through it. They feared the Egyptians would not keep it open to the ships of all countries. So Britain, France, and Israel all attacked Egypt.

The war, however, only lasted a few days, because the United Nations made them all stop

An air view of the
Suez Canal, seen
from the Red Sea

fighting. The Egyptians were allowed to run the Canal themselves, and they ran it very well. They dredged it and made it deeper and wider, so that big modern ships could go through. But still they would not let the Israelis use it. When in 1967, there was war again between Israel and the Arabs, the Canal was blocked, and the short cut to the East was lost to all countries. But today the Canal is not quite so important as it used to be. Oil companies carry much of their oil by pipes across land or in enormous, fast-sailing oil tankers which are too big to go through the Canal, while for passengers aeroplanes are becoming more popular than ships.

38 THE HIGH DAM

The High Dam
being built

WE READ IN Chapter 33 how for centuries the people in Egypt have been dependent on the annual floods of the River Nile for water for growing their crops. Sometimes the floods brought too much water; sometimes not enough. So in 1902 it was decided to build a great dam across the river at Aswan to control the Nile water (see map p. 8). This dam held back much of the flood water in a huge lake, and only let it run on down the river as it was wanted. Many other smaller dams were built all along the Nile valley to hold back water and carry it along irrigation canals to water the fields. But even the Aswan Dam and all these smaller dams were not enough to prevent the Nile flooding in the autumn nor to preserve enough water for the fields in the dry season. So President Nasser decided that a much bigger dam should be built at Aswan.

At first Nasser expected to borrow money from Britain, America, and the World Bank to build his dam, which would take many millions of pounds. But Nasser quarrelled with the Western countries, and they would not lend him money. So he took over the Suez Canal (see Chapter 37) and said he would use the profits from the Canal to build the dam. He also borrowed a great deal of money from Russia. In 1960 he started work on the dam, and many Russian engineers came to Egypt to help.

This dam is so big, one of the biggest dams in the world, that it is called simply The High Dam. All the water which piles up behind it has made a lake about 644 kilometres long by 10 wide, stretching right into the Sudan. About 30,000 men have worked both day and night for many years to build a great pyramid of rock across the river.

They had to work so hard that they had to be excused from fasting during Ramadan, the Muslim month of fasting, and could eat in the middle of the day. The dam is 110 metres high, and a road runs across it. There are six tunnels running through it, with strong steel gates across them. When the gates are opened the water can run through the dam and down the river, but when they are closed, no water can pass.

The great lake behind the dam has drowned thousands of hectares of land in a part of Egypt and the Sudan called Nubia, where there were villages and farms. The Nubian people have been moved to new villages in land which was once desert; but the dam is providing plenty of water to turn the desert into good farm land. Also, as well as drowning villages and fields and trees, the lake has drowned great temples built by the Pharaohs. The greatest of these is the vast temple of Abu Simbel, built 3,000 ears ago by the Pharaoh, Rameses II. The temple was cut into the cliff and in it are four colossal statues of Rameses, so enormous that a man standing between the feet of a statute only reaches up to its ankles. This great temple had been re-discovered and dug out only quite recently. Now it is being buried again —

The statues being moved to safety

under water. So archaeologists from many countries have been working desperately to rescue what they can. The statues of Rameses, enormous as they are, have been cut away from the rock face and taken up to the top of the cliff, above the water.

Now that the High Dam is completed, the Nile will flood no more, and there will be water for irrigation to turn half a million hectares of desert into farms. Also the power of the water can be used to make electricity. With electricity, there can be factories and industries, which will help to make Egypt richer. One of the first of these is a fertilizer factory. In the past the river floods carried rich silt over the country to fertilize the fields each year, but now that there are no floods, there is no silt. So the farmers must have fertilizers instead to make their crops grow.

The Nile Valley, which was one of the earliest parts of the world to be rich and civilized, should become more prosperous again now that man has learnt how to control the great river; and both the Egyptians and the people of the Sudan, who have for so long been poor, should again have better lives.

Giant statues at Abu Simbel, which would have been drowned

39 THE MAGHREB

THE ARABS CALL the lands of North Africa — Libya, Tunisia, Algeria, and Morocco (see map p.8) — the *Maghreb*, which means 'the lands of the west'. This is the part of the Arab world most distant from the Arab heartland — Arabia, and it is different from Arabia in many ways. When the Arabs captured most of the countries of the Arab world, they found people there who were not particularly warlike, and who settled down peacefully under their conquerors and eventually became Arabs too. But in the Maghreb there lived the Berber tribes who were tough and loved fighting, and rebelled against the Arabs time and time again. Finally they settled down to live their own lives in the mountains of the Maghreb, as they still do today, and speak their own language. Many of them have fair hair and blue eyes, unlike the Arabs who are usually dark.

As the lands of the Maghreb are nearer to Europe than other Arab countries, the people there have always had more contact with Europe. In recent times, France ruled Morocco, Algeria, and Tunisia, and the big, modern cities — Casablanca and Tangiers in Morocco, Algiers and Oran in Algeria, and Tunis, the capital of Tunisia — look more French than Arab. Behind these cities is a rich, green plain where olives and grapes grow, the prosperous farms are surrounded by gardens and hedges, and little white French churches stand in the middle of the villages. Now that the French have left, the churches are empty and closed, and storks build their nests on the belfries, for the people of the Maghreb themselves are Muslims. Between the coastal plains and the desert are some magnificent ancient cities, such as Fez, Marrakesh, and Tlemcen, built by the Arabs long ago. The *souqs* (markets) in these cities are like those in Jerusalem or Aleppo, and in spite of all the changes that have come to the Maghreb, these cities have not changed.

Further inland, beyond the plain, is the great range of the Atlas mountains, and a world which is neither French nor Arab. On the high peaks there is snow in winter and spring. Lower down, the land is green, and big brown monkeys live wild there. Berber villages are perched on wild crags in the mountains, where they can protect themselves against warlike neighbours (see Chapter 41).

Beyond the mountains and the fertile plains lies the great Sahara Desert, the biggest desert in the world (see Chapter 3). This is the land of the Tuareg, a fierce people who live wandering lives, rather like the Bedouin (see Chapter 6). They are tall and slender and ride fine horses. They live in small, square tents made of black goat's hair, with coloured stripes, each tribe having its own colours. Although they are Muslims, women have far more liberty than most Muslim women, and in the south it is the men, not the women, who wear veils. They wear a long blue cloth wound round the head to form a hood and then over the face, leaving only a slit for the eyes. Camels are their most important possessions, and in the past they were always making raids on their neighbours to steal camels. They also used to attack caravans crossing the Sahara, and merchants used to have to pay them for protection on the caravan routes. They were great fighters, able to fire their rifles from the backs of galloping horses or camels. But the French, when they came to North Africa, were determined to control the desert themselves, and after many years of fighting, they made the Tuareg submit.

Here and there in the Sahara water is to be found, and in such places oasis towns have been built (see Chapter 5). These towns are very old and differ from each other a great deal, but they all have date groves, which are watered with the precious water pumped up from the wells. When it is very hot, the people of the oasis sleep out at night under the trees. Each family keeps a few chickens and black goats. One goatherd takes all the goats out by day to find fodder in the desert, and at sunset, when they return, each goat runs off through the streets of the town back to its own house. Today the Sahara is changing a great deal, for oil and gas have been found under the desert sand. Teams of workmen have come and built long, straight tarmac roads and pipelines to carry the oil across the desert to the coast. The Sahara is no longer entirely poor and desolate, but the source of great riches.

Moroccan tribesmen and their tents, with a village in the background

40 A DESERT TOWN

Muhammad's home in a desert town in Algeria

AS THE SUN rises over the desert, Muhammad opens his eyes and gets up from the mat on which he has been sleeping. All round him people are beginning to stir: his parents, brothers, sisters, nephews, and nieces. As Muhammad opens the door, sunlight streams into the dark, windowless room in Messaad, a little town in Algeria.

Muhammad goes out into the bare yard to take a drink of water from a goat's skin hanging against the wall. The water is slightly brown and tastes of the tar with which the skin is treated. In the yard the family's goats are waking too, ready to be taken out to the desert hills for the day. Muhammad must hurry because, before going to the village school, he goes to a religious school where he learns to recite the Koran by heart. His mother

gives him a cup of black coffee and some dry bread for breakfast, and then he goes out into the street through the only door in the yard wall.

Muhammad walks along the sandy street which runs between the flat-roofed stone houses. Each house is the same. A doorway opens onto the yard, round which are two or three rooms, usually with no windows at all, certainly with no windows looking onto the street. This is because Muslim women are not allowed to look out of their homes, nor may anyone else look in on them. Muhammad's mother and Fatma, his married 16-year-old sister, and his father's second wife stay at home all the day. If they do go out they must cover themselves from head to toe with a white veil, leaving only one eye peeping out. Only old women and little girls can come and go freely and unveiled in Messaad. Muhammad's 13-year-old sister is free just now, but this summer she will be shut in until her parents have found a husband for her.

Muhammad's father has no work to do, and he spends most of the day sitting on the street in the sun, chatting to the other men who also have no work. Employment is not easy to find in Messaad. Fatma's husband earns a little money building houses in the town, which is growing larger all the time.

When the men have gone out, the women sit down on mats on the floor to work. Muhammad's mother spins a thread of brown wool with a spindle like a spinning top with a long handle, which she turns against her leg. Fatma sits behind a loom with threads stretching right across one end of the room, from floor to ceiling. Her baby lies on the floor beside her, with his head in a big straw hat to keep off the buzzing flies. Fatma is weaving a *burnous*, a hooded shepherd's cloak, which will take months to make. When it is finished, her father will sell it, and the family will have money for food. The second wife grinds corn between two big stones for the family's bread. They chat happily together as they work. The only furniture in the room is a small round table.

The winter is bitterly cold in Messaad, and the wind howls across the desert. Each house has a small fireplace, but there is little wood to burn, and the door must be open, for otherwise the room is too dark; there is no electric light in most houses in Messaad. Everyone shivers with cold, and Muhammad huddles into his small *burnous* and longs for spring.

In summer the sun beats fiercely down on the little town, and the stones and sand are hot to walk on. The children have to look out for scorpions, which sting their feet, and can even kill people. Only the narrow strip of ground in the dried-up river bed, where Muhammad's father has a small garden, is fresh and green. There, tall palm trees wave their feathery leaves above the mud walls, and pomegranates, apricots, and a few vegetables grow. But not many vegetables can be grown because there is so little water.

Muhammad's eldest sister is married to her cousin, a tribesman, who lives in a square, red-and-black striped tent in the desert. In spring, when the tough grass around Messaad is young and green, they come to stay with their relatives in the town. They have two little children. They had two other babies, but one died of cold in the winter, and the other fell ill in the desert, and his parents could not reach the clinic in time. Muhammad's sister says it was the will of Allah, but she hangs charms round the necks of the other two and paints their foreheads black, against the Evil Eye.

The tent-dwelling people take their flocks to the cooler highlands to the north in the summer. In autumn they visit Messaad again on their way further south for the winter. If they have had a good season they bring animals for their relatives

A garden on the outskirts of the town

in Messaad and also buy many things in the market there. Then everyone in the town is happy. But if they have had a bad year some will have so few animals that they will have to stay and live in the town. This means less food for everyone, for the townspeople depend on the nomad herdsmen to bring money to the town. Today, tent-dwelling people are becoming fewer.

41 THE MOUNTAINS OF THE ARAB WORLD

WE THINK OF the Arab World as a land of hot deserts and of big river valleys, such as the Nile Valley and Mesopotamia. But there are also some great mountain ranges, particularly in Morocco and Algeria, in the Lebanon, in the north of Iraq, and in the Yemen in the south of the Arabian Peninsula. In fact, much of the desert is mountainous also, but this is less important because almost no one lives there.

The High Atlas in Morocco

The highest of the Arab mountains are the High Atlas Mountains in Morocco, which reach to nearly 4,270 metres and have snow on them for several months of the year. In these parts of the Arab World there is plenty of rain, for the mountains trap the clouds from the sea. So they are green, and in ancient times they grew great forests. The cedars of Lebanon were particularly famous, but most of them were cut down and taken to Egypt to build the palaces of the Pharaohs. In those days, when people cut down trees, they did not plant more trees, so today most of the forests are gone. But the lower slopes of the mountains have been cut into terraces and planted with fruit trees. The mountain people grow olives and figs, almonds, apples, and mulberries, and many other crops, and bring water to the terraces along little irrigation channels.

The weather in the mountains can be very hot in the summer and bitterly cold in the winter. There are often terrible thunderstorms with torrents of rain. Paths in the mountains can become rivers in a few seconds and violent floods can wash away fields, break down houses, and drown people and animals. But although life can be harsh in the mountains, they can also be a safe refuge from enemies. So in the mountain ranges of the Arab world, non-Arab people have defended themselves against the Arab conquerors and have gone on living their own lives and speaking their own languages in their well-protected mountain villages.

In the High Atlas and Rif Mountains in Morocco, and in the mountains of Algeria, live tribes of Berbers, who retreated there centuries ago when the Arabs invaded their country (see Chapter 39). Their villages are often built on inaccessible crags, the houses huddled close together, presenting blank walls to the outside world and looking like little fortresses. They are built of brown stone and baked mud, with roofs of red tiles. The villagers used to carry on constant feuds between each other, shooting each other and trying to drive each other out. But, when attacked by an outside enemy, they would combine together and present a formidable force. In 1921, for example, the Berbers of Morocco united under a great leader, Abd el Krim, and defeated a large Spanish army and drove it out of the Rif Mountains. After 5 years' fighting, it took a combined Spanish and French army with tanks and aircraft finally to subdue them. In Algeria the war of independence against France was started in the Berber mountains and kept alive there until Algeria finally won her independence in 1962.

In the Lebanon, two minority groups have survived in the mountains: a Christian group and the Druses, a strange sect of Muslims. Although Christians and Druses are now usually peaceful, and many of the villagers come down to the towns to work, feuds still flare up suddenly, and shooting starts between rival families in a village before government troops can restore order.

The mountains of the Kurds

The Kurds are a very warlike and independent people who live in the mountains in the north of Iraq. They have never submitted to being ruled by the Arabs, and to this day are struggling against the Iraq Government demanding to have a separate state of their own. The Kurds are natural fighters: Saladin, the great leader who defeated the Crusaders in the 12th century, was a Kurd (see Chapter 18). And the mountains in which they live are so remote and rugged that the government soldiers find it very difficult to fight there. When they are not fighting, the Kurds are mostly shepherds, and they keep their sheep in great caves during the winter to protect them from the cold.

The Lebanon

The Yemen mountains in the south-west of Arabia were for centuries the home of powerful kingdoms, including that of the Queen of Sheba. The ancient Yemenis carved terraced fields on the slopes of the fertile mountains and grew rich crops. As long ago as 500 years before the birth of Christ, they built a great dam, called the Marib Dam, high in the mountains, and for a thousand years this provided water for irrigating wonderful crops. Everything grew well there, including frankincense and some of the finest coffee in the world. Then an earthquake burst the dam, and the splendid farmlands were ruined. No one repaired the dam, and Yemen sank into a backward and poor mountain state. In 1962 a revolution broke out against the ruler, and for years after, war raged through the high mountain passes of the Yemen.

The Yemen

42 THE ARABIC LANGUAGE

IF YOU WERE to watch an Arab boy reading his comic, you would soon notice that he was reading from back to front and right to left. The lines of his comic printed in Arab would look like this:

An Arabic comic strip.
(right) 'We'll come to the town in a jiffy.'
(left) 'Shouldn't we take some grub with us?' 'No objection.'

Although you might guess that this was writing, you would not be able to make out any of the letters. Actually our alphabetic writing and the Arabic one come from the same origins, which are quite different from Chinese writing, for instance, which does not have an alphabet of our kind. Alphabetic writing was probably invented along the eastern shores of the Mediterranean nearly 4,000 years ago. The Arabs developed their writing from this, and the Phoenician sailors brought it to Europe.

Of course the alphabet has changed a great deal during all its travels, and now the only letter which looks the same in Arabic and English is the 'L', except that it is backwards in Arabic. There are 28 letters in Arabic. There are no capital letters and only three vowels, a, i, and u, and these are written just as little marks above or below the other letters, or usually not written at all. If you were to write 'the little kitten played with his mother' the Arabic way, it would be: 'th lttl kttn plyd wth hs mthr'. When Arabic names are written in English they are often spelled in many different ways, because of the lack of vowels. Muhammad, for instance, is spelt Mahomet or Mohammed; in Arabic it is مُحَمَّد, mhmmd (only read from right to left).

Many ordinary English words were originally Arab words. Sugar and rice, for example, which the Crusaders first tasted in Arab lands, come from the Arabic words *sukar* and *ruz*. Some words came through traders: lemons and cotton, for example, and muslin from Mosul and Damask from Damascus. Amen, alcohol, chemist, giraffe, jar, track, and admiral are all common words which came from Arabic. In the Middle Ages the Arabs were the best scientists in the world, and so we have many scientific Arabic words, such as algebra and chemistry ('al' means 'the' in Arabic).

The Arabs were great mathematicians, and we owe our Arabic numbers to them. They have changed rather since we took them from the Arabs, but some are still a little like the original Arabic ones.

I	II	III	IV	V	VI	VII	VIII	IX	X	Roman
1	2	3	4	5	6	7	8	9	10	English
١	٢	٣	٤	٥	٦	٧	٨	٩	١٠	Arabic

Kufic writing used for decorative and sign writing

Before we started using them we used Roman numbers, many of which needed several figures, such as VIII, for example. There was no zero (0), so you could not write numbers such as 30 (XXX), 300 (CCC), and 3,000 (MMM) by simply adding noughts; multiplication sums could take all day. The Arabs had learnt their numbers in the 8th century from India, and they handed them on to the Spaniards some 200 years later. Soon everyone else in Europe was using them too; they made arithmetic so much easier.

The peoples of all the countries of the Arab world, about 80 million of them, use the Arabic language, and it is a link between them. They are very proud of their language, because they believe it was the language which God spoke when he gave the Koran to Muhammad (see Chapter 10). The language of the Koran is still considered the best Arabic, so Arabs still write the same Arabic as they did 1,300 years ago when the Koran was written. Their speech has changed a little, but their writing has not. When they need new words they make them up out of old ones. For instance, this is

لأول مرة منذ استقالته، خرج الجنرال ديغول
أمس الأول من منزله الريفي وبرفقته زوجته
وذلك للقيام بنزهة في المنطقة القريبة منه
كولومبي لي دوزئغليز. ورافقت الجنرال سيارة
من الحرس . وترجّل الجنرال ديغول وقام
بجولة على الأقدام مع عقيلته .

Everyday Arabic writing, without vowel marks (Ruqa)

what happened when tanks were invented and a word was needed for them. In Arabic there is a word *dab* which means 'to walk slowly, or crawl', and a word *dub* meaning a bear, a creature which lumbers slowly along. So a tank was called a a *dabbaba*, a heavy monster moving slowly but, like the bear, difficult to stop. Sometimes the Arabs have had to give in and accept a foreign word for modern inventions: for example, television in Arabic is also television.

Arabic writing is very beautiful, and has been used as a fine decoration for buildings, pictures, books, and many other objects. The religion of Islam forbids Moslems to use pictures of people or animals in holy places, so artists developed beautiful patterns from letters and lines of writing. A page of the Koran may look more like a picture to us than the page of a book. Indeed, their language is the Arabs' favourite art form.

قَالَ اللهُ تَعَالَى

وَقَضَى رَبُّكَ أَنْ لا تَعْبُدُوا إِلاَّ إِيَّاهُ
وَبِالْوَالِدَيْنِ إِحْسَانًا، إِمَّا يَبْلُغَنَّ عِنْدَكَ
الْكِبَرَ أَحَدُهُمَا أَوْ كِلاهُمَا فَلا تَقُلْ لَهُمَا أُفٍّ
وَلا تَنْهَرْهُمَا وَقُلْ لَهُمَا قَوْلاً كَرِيمًا ۝
وَاخْفِضْ لَهُمَا جَنَاحَ الذُّلِّ مِنَ الرَّحْمَةِ
وَقُلْ رَبِّ ارْحَمْهُمَا كَمَا رَبَّيَانِي صَغِيرًا ۝

Writing with vowel marks, used especially for the Koran (Naskh)

A glazed Islamic tile

A characteristic Arabesque design based on the geometric pattern shown above

WHEN THE ARABS left the deserts after the death of Muhammad, they knew nothing of painting and sculpture, though they had great poets. But they learnt very quickly from the people they conquered. Their first great building, finished only 60 years after Muhammad died, and still considered one of the most beautiful buildings in the world, was the mosque called the Dome of the Rock, in Jerusalem. Its gold-coloured dome shines above the old walls of Jerusalem as though it were new; its walls are covered with mosaic pictures and blue and white tiles (see Chapter 31).

Arab art is mostly concerned with building, pottery, and writing. From the beginning the Arabs devoted much of their best building to making mosques, and much of their best art to decorating these. Because Muhammad had said that they should not make images, they soon came to believe that it was wrong to make pictures or statues of people and even animals. And so instead they developed elaborate patterns to make their walls attractive. The most famous of these patterns we call Arabesque; it was formed of curving stems and leaves of plants, often twining round beautiful Arabic writing. Ornate letters were carved in stone or wood, or more often moulded in plaster, and it is often quite difficult to see that the pattern is writing at all. The Arabs also used this decorated writing for making beautiful copies of the Koran, the Muslim Holy Book.

The towers of Arab mosques, called minarets, are usually very fine. In Cairo they are like long pencils, pointing up to the sky, and some have a bulge at the top. Some are decorated with patterns of brickwork. Inside the mosque is the prayer niche, called the *mihrab*, which faces towards Mecca. Arabs kneel to pray facing the *mihrab*, which is often the most beautifully decorated part of the mosque. Sometimes the ceiling is moulded into row after row of little plaster stalactites, which may be painted in bright colours. Such stalactites are often used on ceilings and arches of other buildings as well as of mosques.

Arabs liked to make many arches in their buildings. They developed a horse-shoe-shaped arch which they often used, and also an arch looking like a clover leaf. In the mosque at Cordoba in Spain they used a forest of arches, piling one row above another. Ordinary Arab houses still often have fine arched windows.

The Court of the Lions
in the Alhambra, Granada

Many Arab rulers built magnificent palaces, in which they used the same kinds of decoration as were in the mosques. Usually the palace would have several courtyards, and in the middle of each courtyard a fountain played. There were even small fountains inside the rooms, for the sound of running water is very refreshing in hot Arab summers. Around the room rugs and cushions of splendid colours and designs were laid for guests to sit on. A very fine example of an Arab palace is the Alhambra, at Granada in southern Spain.

INDEX

Abd al Rahman, 8th-century Arab ruler of Spain, 36
Abd el Krim, 20th-century Berber leader, 88
Aby Bakr, Muhammad's father-in-law and successor, 30
Abu Simbel, ancient Egyptian temple, 82
Aisha, Muhammad's favourite wife, 26
Aladdin, character in *Arabian Nights*, 32
Al Azhar, Islamic University in Cairo, 78
Aleppo, city in Syria, 60
Alexandria, port of Egypt, 78
Algeria, 84, 86; French colony, 54; oil in, 56; mountains of 88
Algiers, capital of Algeria, 84; pirate headquarters, 48; captured by the French, 54
Ali, founder of Shi'ite sect of Islam in 7th century, 30
Ali Baba, character in *Arabian Nights*, 32
Allah, Muslim name for God, 28
almsgiving, rule of Islam, 28
Antioch, town in Syria, captured by Crusaders, 40
Aqaba, Gulf of, 76
Aqaba, Jordan, port on Red Sea, 52
Arabian Nights, the, traditional Arab tales, 32
Arabian Peninsula, 24; *see also* map p. 8
Arabesque, decorative form of Arab art, 92
Arabs, 10; Arab lands, 8; origins of, 24; religion, 28; language, 90; art, 92; desert life, 16; family life, 20, 86; food, 16, 22; hospitality, 22; 7th-century conquests, 30; in Spain, 36; under Turkey, 50; under English and French, 54; dispute with Israel, 64
Arabic language, 90
arak, Lebanese drink, 22
art, Arab, 92; writing, 90
Aswan High Dam, 82, 72
Atlas mountains, North Africa, 88

Baghdad, capital of Iraq, 34, 32; Mongol destruction of, 44
Barbarossa, 16th-century pirate leader, 48; aiding Turks, 50
Barbary pirates, 48
Basra, port of Iraq, 47
Bedouin, desert-dwellers, 18, 12, 25; with Lawrence of Arabia, 52
Beirut, capital of Lebanon, 70
Berbers, peoples of North Africa, 88
Bethlehem, town in Jordan, 66
bilharzia, disease of Nile valley peasants, 74
Blue Nile, tributary of Nile, 72
British rule of the Arabs, 54

Cairo, capital of Egypt, 78
Caliph, a Muslim chief ruler, 30
Calvary, scene of Christ's crucifixion, 68
camels, 18, 24
camel caravans, 38
canals: for transport: built by Saladin, 42; Suez Canal, 80. *See also* irrigation

caravan routes, 38, 60; *see also* map p. 8
caravans, 38, 14, 24
Casablanca, chief port of Morocco, 84
Cedars of Lebanon, 88
child care, in Arab village, 74, 86
Children's Crusade, 40
Christians: home of Christ, 64, 66; Crusades, 40; in Lebanon, 71, 89; *see also* Book 15
Church of the Holy Sepulchre, Jerusalem, 68
clothing, Arab, 10
coffee-drinking, 22
Constantinople (Istanbul), city in Turkey, 50; Christian Emperor of, 40
Cordoba, Arab city in Spain, 36; cathedral of, 92
couscous, North-African spicy mutton stew, 22
Crusades, the, 40, 42

Dakhla, oasis town in Egypt, 16
Damascus, capital of Syria, 34; sacked by Mongols, 44
Damascus Gate, of Jerusalem, 68
dams: on Tigris and Euphrates rivers, 46; at Aswan, Egypt, 82, in ancient Yemen, 88
date plams, 16; in Iraq, 46
Dead Sea, 58
desert, 12, 14; people of, 18, 24; Berbers and Taureg, 84; oases in, 16; travel in, 38; desert town, 86; oil in, 56
desert travel, 38, 14, 22
dhows, shallow Arab boats, 48
Dome of the Rock, the, mosque in Jerusalem, 64, 68
Druses, Lebanese sect of Muslims, 88

Egypt: village life, 74; cities, 78; under British, 54; under Nasser, 76; the Nile Valley, 72; the High Dam, 82; Suez Canal, 80
Eilat, Israeli port on Gulf of Aqaba, 76
electricity, making of, 82; *see also* Book 20
Empty Quarter, Arabia, 14, 12
Euphrates river, Iraq, 46; *see also* Fertile Crescent
Evil Eye, Arab belief in, 74, 86

factories: paper factories in Cordoba, 36; fertilizer factories in Egypt, 82
Faisal, king of Iraq after 1st World War, 52
family, Arab, 20; in Egyptian village, 74; in Algeria, 86
farming: in oases, 16; in Mesopotamia, 46, 58; in Jordan valley, 58; in Nile Valley, 72, 74; terrace farming in mountains, 58, 88; *see also* irrigation
Farouk, last king of Egypt, 76
fasting, rule of Islam, 28
fellahin, Egyptian peasants, 74, 10
felucca, sailing boat on Nile, 72
fennec, desert fox, 14
Fertile Crescent, 58
Fez, city in Morocco, 84